o/s

GW00383972

The Very Merry ~~Widow~~ MOIRA

Moira Lister

The Very Merry ~~Widow~~ MOIRA

HODDER AND STOUGHTON

Printed in Great Britain
for Hodder and Stoughton Limited,
St. Paul's House, Warwick Lane, London, E.C.4,
by Richard Clay (The Chaucer Press), Ltd.,
Bungay, Suffolk

Foreword

MISS LISTER reveals in this book that – when she heard that I was to co-star with her in a comedy called *The Gazebo* a few years ago – she was, to put it mildly, worried about me. I can only reveal in return that I was absolutely petrified of her. The play had been running with great success for several months at the Savoy, and I was asked to take over from Ian Carmichael, who was leaving to make a film. I had never met Miss Lister, but I could well understand her qualms. It may not have been noticed by the theatre-going public, but I am neither the same shape nor age-group as Mr. Carmichael. One other quite minor point – the fact that it was the first time I had ever appeared professionally on any stage, let alone in a starring role in the West End, cannot, I feel, have given my leading lady any great confidence. For my part, I had always thought of Moira as the acme of glamour and sophistication: invariably exquisitely dressed and groomed, constantly photographed looking dazzling at first nights and high society functions, with a house in Belgravia and a villa in the South of France, and all that jazz. And in private life wasn't she a Vicomtesse or something? Long before we met, I had decided that rapport was out. I don't go to first nights or high society functions, I am given to sweaters and slacks that should really have been sent to the cleaners weeks ago, and my nearest approach to the aristocracy is reading the Earl of Arran in the *Evening News*.

I rehearsed, of course, with the understudies. On my last run-through before the actual take-over ordeal, I saw to my horror – sitting in the front row of the stalls – a very light, almost white, fur coat and above it that glorious mane of blonde hair. She sat alone in the theare, with her arms folded, and not a muscle moved, not a sound was heard, not a funeral note apart from the sound of my own voice ploughing through the lines, by now convinced that in the ploughing I was digging – had already dug – my theatrical grave. We got through my first night somehow, and the following afternoon yet another rehearsal was called. It was all too obvious that it had been called for me and me alone, and gradually it dawned even on my impaired intellect that there had been a number of occasions during the drama when I was in not exactly the right position *vis-à-vis* the leading lady. After about the seventy-fourth request from the director to move a little nearer to the footlights, I plucked up courage to say to Miss Lister, "D'you mean I'm up-staging you?" "Yes, dear," she said. "And for someone who's never been on the stage before, you're far too good at it. Now let's go over to the Savoy and have a zonking great drink." Since when she has become my dearest and greatest friend. If the Vicomte will skip this next line, I love her.

The opening skirmishes of *The Gazebo* over, Moira settled in more or less permanently in my dressing room and I don't think that for a single moment in all those months we ever stopped laughing. Except, of course, when on stage. Well, come to think of it, on certain occasions not even there. I am very happy to know that, all these years later, we are still together – and still laughing. She is, as is evident in reading this book, the complete one-hundred-per-cent professional: and at the same time, provided she is not saddled with people who are *not* professional, she manages to get fun out of her work. She has the most enormous energy and capacity for both work and play: behind all that glamour I feel there is a tennis champion or an Olympic Games swimming gold-medallist bursting to get out. Two or three years ago, we spent a holiday together at Èze on the Côte d'Azur. There was a raft moored about two hundred yards off the beach, and she beat me to it

6

by about fifty yards five times a day. It was very annoying: I got quite piqued. No one looking as glamorous as that should have so powerful a crawl-stroke, and no really distinguished (if podgy) playwright should be seen plodding away at the breast-stroke all that distance behind.

Our relationship over the years has been unusual, and always fun. I started as Moira's husband in *The Gazebo*: she is now my widow on B.B.C. TV. The star of a regular weekly series such as *The Very Merry Widow* has no easy life. Five days' rehearsal only to get a big part under your belt; filming on location on your one day off; the strain of putting one episode in the can on one evening each week, and turning up at ten o'clock the following morning in some remote Church Hall or Youth Club to start work on the next. You have to do your homework when you're at home, and be permanently on the ball in the rehearsal room or the studio. Moira does both, and by some fortunate metabolism manages to remain fun and to look a million dollars at the same time. She also, of course, manages to find time to appear on the stage, in films, on sound radio, to be the most wonderful mother, and to knock off a book like this in her spare time. With all respect to Milton Shulman, Peter Black and the rest of them, the true television critics are the boys on the studio floor: the camera, sound and lighting crews, the floor managers, the scene-shifters and so on. Halfway through the last *Very Merry Widow* series, one of these admirable characters came up to me in the studio, pointed across to where Moira was giving her all and said, "She's great to work with, isn't she, guv'nor?"

In very real gratitude for the years we have worked together, I agree. She's great to work with.

ALAN MELVILLE

Illustrations

Frontispiece[1]

facing page

The first picture taken of me professionally, aged eleven 14

Myself in 1947, my first look at the Vicomte! 14

The great day, my wedding – December 23rd, 1951[2] 14

Chantal's christening, October 19th, 1954 15

The Love of Four Colonels. The ideal of four colonels and my ideal role 48

Peter Ustinov, father and creator of the four colonels 49

Douglas Fairbanks, a real colonel and a dish![3] 49

World Tour programme of *People in Love* – Noel Coward, Sir John Gielgud, Tyrone Power, Peter Ustinov, Bob Hope, Maurice Chevalier! 64

Holloway Jail. My first really captive audience! 65

I played to every available audience in South Africa![4] 96

Jacques, Chantal and myself in South Africa[5] 96

My orchestral debut at the Albert Hall – four notes as a nightingale![6] 97

Enter Christobel. Godmama, The Duchess of Rutland[7] 112

Children dancing at piano at home[8] 112

Bob Hope: "Shall I kiss you now or shall I tease you a little first?"[9] 113

Rex Harrison[10] 113

Moments I treasure most[11] 144

9

Ian Carmichael   145

Derek Nimmo[12]   145

Yul Brynner in *The Double Man*   160

The Very Merry Widow, Alan Melville style[13]   160

The Very Merry Widow in action and How![14]   161

[1] Jon Lyon, Rex Features Ltd.
[2] Baron
[3] Douglas Fairbanks Ltd.
[4] Aztec Services Pty. Ltd.
[5] Photo-Hausmann
[6] *The Evening News*
[7] Barry Swaebe
[8] John D. Drysdale
[9] Matthews' News and Photo Agency
[10] Norman Hargood
[11] *London Express*
[12] Charel P. Pienaar
[13] B.B.C. television
[14] Joan Williams

Chapter 1

THE first recollection of my entry into the theatrical world was a nightmare – an actual nightmare, not a metaphorical one. It was the eve of my debut at the umbilical age of six in a play by Ibsen called *The Vikings of Helgeland*. After our dress rehearsal I had been put to bed in the room of my elocution teacher as it was too far for me to return to our farm in the untrammelled veldt of the Transvaal. Almost immediately my head touched the pillow began the first of a long series of repetitive dreams that were to plague me for the rest of my life – commonly known as the actor's dream. You are on a stage alone and the house is sold out, you are standing in the wings waiting to go on, your conscience is chastising you for not having done more work on your role, then suddenly you are thrust on to the stage and you know the moment of truth has come. You open your mouth to give the performance of your life – and nothing happens. Your throat is dry, your mind a blank, your knees knocking and your heart banging to bursting point. Titters come from the audience, softly at first then in increasing volume and as the noise gains momentum so does slow hand-clapping become louder and faster, then jeering then booing, until one looks at oneself to find every strip of clothing has vanished, and one is standing stark naked in front of a vast sea of faces. Panic sets in and you try to leave the stage but suddenly the sets hem you in and you can't move, hysteria grips you and you start to scream – at that moment if you're lucky someone wakes you up or, as happened that first time, I had actually left my bed and was crouching between the wardrobe and the wall trying desparately to get out. There my teacher found me and carried me back to her bed where I spent the rest of the night burying myself in her more than maternal bosom.

Now I'm sure that Freud would have a highly complicated explanation for that. But for me it's simply something with which I've learned to live as part and parcel of a demanding career, which expects no less than a wholehearted attempt at perfection. And indeed the next day all was forgotten when I read my name in print for the first time and received my first accolade, which read, "The sweet face and voice of little Moira Lister was as music amid the tragic scenes of Helgeland." I was hooked. It was enough to decide me to devote the rest of my days – dreams or not – to pursuing the acclaim of public and press to my interpretation of whatever role I was lucky enough to be allowed to create.

I don't remember much about that first part, being only six years old, except that I was a prince which appealed to my vivid imagination, and that I had some very moving scenes where I was torn away from my mother. And as I was devoted to my own mother it was not very difficult for me to imagine how devastating it would be if anyone tried to wrench me away from her.

My beautiful mother, had she lived in our permissive society, would have been a great actress. But her mother having the strictures of a whale-boned Victorian Scottish up-bringing, was horrified when she discovered my mother had got herself a starring role in a silent film – and went down and accused the perfectly innocuous producer of abducting her daughter; and that if she was not returned home immediately, she would set the police on to the whole enterprise. My mother was delivered back home in a trice. But neither her talent nor her fascination for the arts ever left her and when she gave birth to three buxom daughters at regular intervals of three years, she decided post-haste to sublimate all her frustrations in the three of us. My eldest sister Doreen was trained as a dancer.

In due course she appeared in a film called *Evergreen* with Jessie Matthews, and after this she was offered a Hollywood contract but preferred love and marriage in South Africa. My second sister Evelyn was trained as a pianist, became a composer, subsequently chose love and marriage and lived happily ever after; and I was trained in the dramatic arts and have been experiencing big and little dramas ever since. But quite sure of one emotion, and that is that I am irrevocably tied to the apron strings of probably the most demanding of all lovers, Mr. Theatre.

There was, of course, my father who was trying to persuade us to turn into useful citizens of our adopted country South Africa, but thank heaven my mother was filling our heads with dreams and hopes and aspirations which had no relation to reality at all. And yet she somehow managed to make them come true. We never had a great deal of money but my father, who was by then dabbling in property, sold a house and she took a thousand pounds out of it – I never knew whether it was the profit or the loss – and sailed to England with the three girls and an aunt delightedly trailing behind her determined footsteps, and stayed there for a whole year. I was eleven by then and she thought nothing of keeping us out of school for all that time simply to further our creative arts education. She put me to study with Jack Hulbert's father, Professor Hulbert, who had brought up both Jack and Claude on Shakespeare and for ballet no less than Lydia Kyasht, Russian ballerina. It was important to know how to move, Mother said. We all had the most wonderful time.

It was 1935, when London was at its height after the depression of 1929 and before the war which was to destroy it four years later. My eldest sister who was just eighteen and a great beauty was whisked into a whirl of Hunt balls, which were terribly "in" at that time, and white tie and tails were all *de rigueur*. I used to watch her dress every night, revelling in the excitement, was allowed to hand her her make-up as it went

13

on thick and fast, and rushed to hide myself where I could see her dashing escort arrive looking almost as devastating as she did. Then as soon as they had gone my next sister, Evelyn, aged fifteen, and I used to go straight to her dressing table and make up our own faces and dress ourselves up in bedspreads and her high-heeled shoes and make our own ball at home. We saw the Jubilee which was like a thousand and one nights come true with all the gold coaches and the diamonds and ostrich plumes, and the Indian Princes sailing down the Mall on their heavily jewel-encrusted elephants. We'd seen ostriches and elephants at home but never looking as glamorous as these. So for a whole year we enjoyed all the fabulous sights London had to offer: the Boat Race, the Eton Wall Game, the Derby, Wimbledon, Lords and all the "musts" of the season. I remember my god-father, Walter Frampton's, breakfast table; he was the recorder of Chichester, and a lovely, cuddly white-haired man. They say he was a demon on the bench but to me he was a doll. We stayed in his vast house with the starch-trimmed maids bustling about and the breakfast table groaned under the weight of pheasant, roast beef, sausages, kippers, eggs fried, scrambled, boiled, haddock, and of course porridge, peaches, grapes and figs. Not a bad start to the day.

And so the fun went on until sadly one day my mother announced the money had come to an end. So we trekked back to South Africa. Reluctantly we went back to school, but it was purely secondary in importance. It was about this time, now aged twelve, that I gave a piano recital. Chopin, no less. I can't think what it could have been like as I can hardly play a note today, but I imagine it was arranged by Mother so as not to give me an inferiority complex in the face of the remarkable strides made by my pianist middle sister. But I would have said "yes" to doing practically anything as long as it meant I could get up on a stage. Then the next year my first big break occurred as Sir Seymour Hicks was coming out to South Africa with a repertoire of three plays and needed a child actress for two of

The first picture taken of me professionally, aged
eleven, in London

Myself in 1947, my first look at the Vicomte!

The great day, my wedding – 23rd
December 1951

Chantal's christening, 19th October 1954. A slip of the tongue and the eighty-year-old bishop turned Chantal into Chanel No. 5. Godmother, the Duchess of Sutherland, Godfather Lord Kilmarnock

them. I auditioned and got the part. At last I was in the real legitimate theatre. Staying away from school for rehearsals, then, while playing, going to school, coming home, having a rest, then being driven to the theatre by an elated and shining mother, who acted every word with me every night. Sir Seymour had a rakish reputation among the girls. He was supposed to flit from one to another like a hungry leprechaun. There were great whisperings and conjectures about how many girls he had "touched with his fairy magic". And a veil was quickly drawn over what price they may have had to pay for their fame. Whether any or all of it was true I was sublimely ignorant. That he used to send for me before the show or during the interval and sit me on his lap and feed me with chocolates may have had some ethereal connotation as far as he was concerned, but this must have been disconcerted by my appreciation of the chocolates and the rapt attention which I gave his stories of the theatre. But looking back on it now after years of working with actors who are undoubtedly a very special and wonderful race, he was probably an over-exuberant and flamboyant personality on the surface and underneath as frightened and faithful as the next man.

After the run was over in South Africa, he persuaded my mother to bring me over to London because he had written a film script called *Mr. and Mrs. King* and wanted me to play Mrs. King as a child.

This time my mother dipped into what must certainly have been the loss account and took another thousand pounds and away just the two of us sailed on the same ship as Sir Seymour and his delicately beautiful wife Ellaline Terriss.

However, the voyage was not a very happy one as the company split into two camps and hot temperaments flew from one deck to another. His leading lady, who I believe thwarted his advances as she had just landed a very large financial fish in Johannesburg, and I imagine wanted to remain "pure and palely loitering" until the nuptuals, became his bitter enemy, and his retaliation came in the form of a third-class ticket for her from Liverpool to London instead of the contractual "first". She in turn countered by going to every window on the entire length of the train saying, "Look what this old so-and-so has done to me. I am young and beautiful, he has one foot in the grave. I'll be a great star when he's dead and gone." By a curious stroke of fate she died two years later, aged twenty-seven, giving birth to twins and Sir Seymour lived over another twenty successful and spirited years.

Unfortunately the film he had written was a sort of skit on royalty and the day after we arrived in England King Edward abdicated, so the film was banned. Only last year I had occasion to spend the weekend in the same house-party in Germany as the Duke and Duchess of Windsor and I told him that "his decision almost cost me my theatrical career". He smiled wickedly and said, "That makes two of us."

So there we were in London with no project and an empty void looming rather nastily in front of us. This was our first setback. It was rather a shock. We had envisaged only success. But little five-foot-three-inch Molly Hogan, my mother, was not one to sit down under any such catastrophe. She asked Sir Seymour for a good agent. He kindly recommended his own, and off she marched me to impress him into taking me on his books. Because of Sir Seymour's word I was taken rather on sufferance and without much hope of any jobs. But before long a child actress was needed in an American play being put on which had been a "smash" on the other side. I auditioned and got the part which had a lot of action but not a spoken word. This I adored because it meant I could mime all my thoughts and think fairly different thoughts each night without anyone knowing. I was paid the princely sum of six guineas a week. We started rehearsals with a very strong cast, with the American comedian Percy Kilbride as the star, with Louise Hampton, Mary Merrall and James Stevenson in hot collusion. Rehearsals were a riot with Mr. K. imposing every bit of comedy business which had "gone like a bomb" in the States – and saying every few lines "Wait! you gotta wait here! – there's a big laf! Don't ride thro' the lafs – This'll slay 'em. This is where they fall out of their seats." Unfortunately the play opened six weeks later – to stony silence. Not a laugh, not a giggle, proving once again that the American humour and English appreciation of it is not always a happy marriage. Basically they are poles apart, and the mercurial quality of the American wit disappears when the Englishman dismisses it with a dry and patronising shrug as not very funny. Poor little Percy was destroyed; he never understood why we closed a month later. Still in stony silence.

Once again the magical door had shut in our faces. This was not in our book at all. Where to turn from here? We decided the best thing would be to go to the R.A.D.A., through which it appeared all doors would open. I was now maturing fast to the sensitive age of fourteen. Sir Kenneth Barnes, the principal, indulgently sat through my rendering of Juliet's Balcony Scene, rehearsed, of course, with Mother playing Romeo! And although he admitted that my performance had a certain quality he was not prepared to admit me to the Academy on the pretext that I was too young and too impressionable and that I would end up by losing my individuality and become a carbon copy of the older students. Yet again we were back to square one in our little flat with our money dwindling fast and unable to enter into that faerie world which seemed to tingle just outside our grasp. Several more weeks of banging on unrelenting doors, disquieting letters from home and the gradual realisation that the empyrean road to neon lights and fame and fortune was not a welcoming one to the uninitiated and unequipped and where Lady Luck did not extend her favours lightly. So we silently packed our bags and sailed forlornly from the streets that we were so sure were going to be paved with gold and back to the bush and anonymity of darkest Africa.

Chapter 2

THIS was now my fourth time of crossing the equator. The first time to and from England was just as a little girl of eleven having fun and winning the fancy-dress prize as Mae West with two outsize grapefruits stuffed into someone's black bra and draped with someone else's sequined evening dress, everyone else's costume jewellery, a long cigarette-holder, a large black hat, high-heeled shoes, and parading up and down using my eleven-year-old deep sexy voice to say, "Come up and see me some time," repeatedly until I was given the prize.

The next trip to England aged thirteen was already much more purposeful. I had been en route to what I thought was going to be the launching pad of my meteoric rise to stardom. And this present trip back home was a wiser, sadder and maturer fourteen year old who had already tasted a modicum of both success and failure.

But as I stepped on to that liner I knew that this voyage was not the last one I was going to make. I had decided very definitely that the right thing to do was to finish my education, a necessary adjunct if my career didn't materialise, and I would have something to fall back on. As soon as my schooling was over I would take any job and save to get my fare back to England. Little did I realise that two years later the war would break out and that the next journey would be on a troop-ship in the height of the battle of the Atlantic.

But now there were three peaceful weeks to be spent on board ship, so I cast an eye around to see if there was anyone my age with whom to play the usual orderly games. Yes, there was a boy of exactly fourteen and we teamed up and all went swimmingly for the first week. Then one evening after dinner we were strolling along the deck. It was a sweet and warm night. We were nearing the Canaries and the seagulls were making a pretty white pattern against the darkening sky just above the phosphorescent waves of the wake. We stopped to watch this for a little while until I was conscious of him looking at me very intently. I didn't quite know what to do. I swallowed and cleared my throat, thinking hard of something to say. But nothing came. And then I felt his hand take mine in his and hold it so tight that it hurt. I gave a little yelp and he said, "I'm sorry but I love you terribly." And then he careered off down the deck with all the loneliness of a long-distance runner and disappeared out of sight. I was completely over-come. I wanted desperately to run after him but I was too shy, so I just sat straight down on the deck where I was and buried my head in my knees and felt a wonderful warm glow flood all over me. And although I had not yet reached the interesting state of womanhood, I was old enough to realise that this was the first real emotion I had felt, and that when I became a great actress, which I was fully determined to become, it would be from these depths or heights that I would find my inspira-tion when I would be asked to play Juliet or Desdemona. Never doubting for a moment that I would be asked to play them!

The next day he didn't appear at all and by the evening I was in a great turmoil of desire just to see him and be with him. I asked his mother where he was and she said he wasn't very well and was in his cabin. I asked permission to go and see him. It was given. I tore down the deck to his cabin and when I got to the door I felt foolish and out of place. Eventually, after arguing with myself for what seemed an eternity, I timidly knocked on the door. There was no reply, so I gently pushed open the door. There he was with his head buried in the pillow. I went into the cabin and closed the door. I saw him give a quick surreptitious look and then he said, "Go away – I don't want you to come here and laugh at me." I felt my eyes begin to sting and I just managed a very small voice with which to say, "Please let me stay. I'll never ever laugh at you. I promise." "Well all right," he said rather grudgingly. "Do you want a liquorice?" So peace was restored and I stayed.

After that almost every afternoon we used to go to his cabin and either read or lie on the bunks and talk of our aspirations and ideals, and gradually a love grew between us so tender and of a purity which can only be born of innocence. I would sometimes lie in his arms and we would swear undying love but further than that there was nothing – no fumblings or gropings or caressings, just sublimely happy to be in one another's company. The voyage came to an end and with great heart-tearings we went back to our respective schools – I in Johannesburg and he in Natal. Within a matter of days I received the most beautiful letter from him with all the things I wanted to hear. I immediately put my love and thoughts and memories down on paper and sent it by return to his boarding school; and waited hourly for his answer. It never came. Total, utter and inexplicable silence. Days, weeks and months went by and no word. My poor little heart bled and wept and wailed. But I never heard from him again.

Twenty years elapsed and I was giving a performance in Natal, and at a reception afterwards there was a face in the crowd that I felt I'd seen somewhere before. We were eventually introduced and I was brought face to face with my first love. I could not help but smile to see him now, aged thirty-five, extremely handsome if not quite tall enough and with perhaps just the beginnings of good living beginning to show, but with a very pretty wife at his side. He said, "Of course I knew who you were but I didn't think you'd remember me." "Remember you!" I said, "You owe me a letter!" He laughed and told me the story of what had happened. My letter had fallen into the hands of the headmaster, who had read it and found it far too full of love and imagination, and had sent it straight to his father, threatening expulsion if this sort of thing continued. The father got straight into his car, drove one hundred miles to the school. Without a word of explanation to the boy, drove him home in silence, then dragged him into his study, took his sjambok (a sort of Zulu cat-o'-nine-tails) off the wall and thrashed the daylights out of him, and said. "That'll teach you to fill your head with girls at your age." Then he put him back in the car and drove back the one hundred miles in silence and left him at the school.

With permission of his wife who was leaving for the country next day with his two children, he asked me to dine with him the following night. We spent that evening reminiscing and filling in each other's twenty years. We both ended up in tears. We danced till five a.m., then he drove me back to my hotel as the tropical dawn was breaking over the sugar-cane fields with the deep Indian Ocean bringing down a suitable backcloth to our last scene – we will probably never meet again. The following week I received this letter:

"Moira darling

"It is probable you are surprised I have not written sooner, and well you should be, as I have put pen to paper many times but never had the courage to post the results of my endeavours. They have ranged from long ramblings of devotion to brief notes suggesting when would be convenient for me to visit Johannesburg. I feel awkward and gauche and my pen will not follow the dictates of my heart and mind – and my efforts are, even now, followed by long moments of indecision.

"Much of what I feel is instinctive, as few men could travel so far through life and suddenly meet the Past with such impact, as I felt when I met you again. As I write this letter to you tonight the past is mainly rolled away in so much as I can still feel the deep devotion I had when I wrote my first love letter, so many years ago. I know it seems ridiculous to imagine that love can exist through eternity, but perhaps that is what I really do believe. The first stirring of love I ever had was for you, and for many years as an adolescent I carried your image in my heart, and then as Time heals – as it must heal all things – it blurred your image. So you became a symbol of what I sought. I tell you this in the hope that you will the better be able to understand why I told you about my past. Why I write to you now and above all why I am so devoted to you. Irrespective of the past, present or future I am glad to know that to have faith and belief is, in the end, worth while. I would rather believe in perfection and continually strive for the ideal than accept the everyday substitute.

"To me, as I write tonight, I cannot but wonder what would have happened if our paths had run parallel, but perhaps it is just as well fate does what it does with us, as in the ultimate rending of accounts we are unable to affect the settlement – however, of one thing I am sure – my first love letter, written as it was with pure heart and humble mind, was probably more nearly the truth than I ever realised, and was certainly well worth the beating it unjustly deserved!! To know that an ideal is still perfect makes up for much, and to know that instinct was both innocent and right will give me warmth and faith through the years to come. If you feel in any degree as I do, you must agree that love, as I feel for you, is not a material thing of passion, nor limited by time, but something near to complete faith and perfection – and for all this, and our reunion, I give you great and hearty thanks.

"You are, and always will be, what no other woman can ever be – my first and only true love.

"My love to you.

"Michael."

I knew that our lives had grown too far apart and it was too dangerous to try to rekindle old emotions through which new ones would flourish, and although I was deeply grateful for his letter I didn't pursue it. I'm sure he realised why and understood.

Well, the next two years from fourteen to sixteen were filled with cramming the lost years into passing my school-leaving exam. Unfortunately, in the last week of exams I was cast as the Queen of the Under Sea Ballet! So I wrote my history paper, a three-hour paper, from eight to ten, then I feigned illness and went straight to rehearsals at ten-thirty a.m. I didn't mind missing an hour of my history paper but I was determined not to be late for rehearsal. This was a big imported spectacular. It was a great experience and wondrous fun. I loved the music and have wanted to do a musical ever since. One of my unfulfilled ambitions. Not that I have a note in my head, but being a firm believer in the fact that one can achieve anything on this earth if you want it enough, I feel that if I really worked at it maybe I could!

It was during a performance one evening about this time that I first heard the word Lesbian. Having had a strict convent Catholic education, it was not a word I had heard bandied about. I was waiting to make my entrance with the principal boy who was in fact a very buxom lady with a lovely voice who shall be nameless. The principal girl, who had better also be nameless, was a delicate milk-and-honey beauty who was, it seemed, inseparable from her principal boy. But both of them, having been imported from overseas were new challenges for the local squires to conquer, and the principal girl was being inundated with offers and offerings. The buxom principal boy was probably not doing quite so well, so was driven to remark to me as we were going on stage, "It really makes me die with laughter when I see these men making such fools of themselves over her, because of course we're Lesbians." I had no idea what she meant but not wanting to appear ignorant, I said, "Oh, how lovely for you!" When I got home that night I couldn't quite remember the word, so I tried to ask my mother what it meant when two women

23

didn't like men because they were something beginning with "L". She of course had no intention of explaining it to me and simply said, "Poor things, just don't go too near them, dear." I was naturally convinced they had a mild form of leprosy and avoided them as much as I could from then on.

At the end of that year I turned seventeen. War had broken out, but it was so remote from us in South Africa that it didn't make much impact. Not to me at any rate. I had no brothers, but Daddy of course joined up again, and was a Major and looked very impressive in his uniform. He was stationed in Pretoria, so came home every weekend.

It was about this time that enormous convoys started to pass through Durban. Forty-five thousand men would arrive and stay from three days to three weeks and then leave for unknown destinations. This was a time of great excitement for all the eligible girls and uneligible ones too. The choice was endless. Parties were continuous and the hospitality unrivalled. I would like to wager there is hardly a man who passed through Cape Town or Durban at that time who hasn't a wonderful memory tucked away somewhere.

I happened at that time to spend a short holiday with my sisters and mother in Durban. We were invited to a party where there were some charming English cavalry officers. I was introduced and among them was a particularly shy Major. I was pretty shy myself, saving all my extrovert inclinations for when I was on stage, so we got talking. And during the course of conversation, he said, "When this is all over and you are in England, my mother and I would be delighted if you would spend a quiet weekend with us in Somerset." And he gave me his address. He left the next day for the North. Little did I know that that name and address were going to be about the most important in my life. However, the moment had not yet arrived, so I returned to Johannesburg and started to take day-time jobs to augment the few pounds I earned acting at night. The first one was selling gramophone records. But as I got so carried away every time I played some classical work, I regret that twice I rather crossly chastised a customer for talking while the music was playing, saying that it was sacrilege, and she didn't deserve to own the records. I was sacked, but for quite another reason. I couldn't bear to wear shoes while the music was playing. It's some sort of strange quirk I have, a sort of yearning for freedom or something like that. The boss walked in one day and saw me serving with no shoes on. I was very soon out on the street, with my shoes following very closely behind! The next job was a tremendous success – selling dresses in a basement shop in Johannesburg. My turnover was enormous because I gave a superb performance with each new customer, telling her how fantastic she looked in each dress she tried on. My sales talk flowed, my flattery fell like silk off a loom, and by the time I'd finished the customer felt like the most beautiful woman who had ever walked into the store: and so bought far more than she had ever intended. But once I'd played the part for a month, I got restless and decided to leave, but the owners had been so kind to me that I didn't want to hurt them by just walking out, so I had to invent a good story. This I never found difficult. So one morning I went to work with a face right out of my make-up box. Very pale, pale purple rings under my eyes, very pale lipstick, dark shadow on my lids and very short of breath with a hard dry cough. I struggled bravely through the morning, coughing between customers, sitting down in breaks, until the owner called me to his office and asked if I were unwell. Tears filled my eyes, and I hesitantly said I was afraid that I would have to leave, because working in a basement with the lack of air was only encouraging the disease of which I would probably die eventually, like all my family had, consumption. I did a quick faint and after being revived with a drop of brandy I was helped up the stairs into a bright light world with two months' money in an envelope. I hasten to add that my family are disgustingly healthy and are still, thank God, very much with me, except for my

25

beloved mother who died of something other than consumption.

My third and last attempt in the world of commerce was as a book-keeper. I answered an advertisement in the leading paper, which said, "Book-keeper required for large store, etc." Well, I wasn't bad at the convent at book-keeping, so I thought I could probably tackle it, but it was the salary that enticed me. It was enormous – twenty-five pounds per month. I worked out that if I could stay there for five months it would pay my fare to England and give me a few pounds to live on till I got back into the theatre. So I put on my most suitable austere attire, nothing frivolous for a book-keeper, and marched down to a store about the size of Swan and Edgars. Very confidently, because now I was playing a part of a highly competent book-keeper, I sat in front of the director, and everything he asked me I answered pat. I said Yes to everything in connection with the work. I knew it all and he needn't worry about a thing, just leave everything to me. Naturally I got the job. I was shown into a plush office where an old Scottish lady who had held the job for thirty years was retiring. She would help me, he said, and left us nose to nose.

Madame Haggis took an instant dislike to me and refused to show me one single thing. Not that I'd have understood if she had. And she put her Scottish nose in the air, upped and left me. I sat in that office for three days, not knowing what to do or where to start. I don't think I even opened one of the books, they looked so different even on the outside to the ones I had used at school. Until on Friday afternoon I looked up to see a queue of forty-five women dressed in black and white standing at my door. I was horrified when I realised they had come to me for their wages. I grabbed my hat and coat, ran down to the director's office and said, "Please, please forgive me, but if you don't want your books absolutely ruined, and to lose your entire restaurant staff, please sack me now." I noticed a quick mental struggle on his part between giving up what I think he thought might have developed into an interesting association, and the ruination of his business. And being a practical man, he graciously sacked me. And to my great surprise, I left with three days' salary in an envelope.

Well, after those three attempts at earning money outside of the theatre, I was never foolish enough to attempt it again. I threw myself wholeheartedly into whatever radio or theatre work there was. I played in *Quiet Wedding* and was desperately upset one night when I overheard two soldiers talking about me outside my dressing-room window, having just seen the show. All I heard was, "Well, she could pee in my soup any day." I burst into floods of tears, taking it as terribly insulting and lacking in respect. It was only years later I realised that it was meant as a compliment.

The next play was a Ralph Lynn farce called *Tons of Money*. One night when I was just reaching the climax of my comedy scene, one of the other actors who was not on stage had felt peckish and ordered fish and chips from the café next door, and to my horror an enormous native boy in a chef's hat got slightly lost among the back-stage flats and walked straight across the stage bearing his tray before him, bowed and said, "Sacabona, missie," and exited the other side. The audience laughed so much that we were very tempted to offer the actor a free dinner every night, provided it could be served in the same way.

It was at this time that Ivor Novello's producer of *The Dancing Years* and the great German success *Mädchen in Uniform* came out to South Africa. Leontine Sagan. She was a tall, statuesque masculine figure, Germanic, demanding, cruel, but a great task-master. She centred on me like a Svengali with a victim. She whipped me into shape, humiliated me, ridiculed me, then built me up and cosseted me until she could wring out of me the performance she wanted to get. I became the lead of all the plays she did – two plays by a local playwright Madeleine Masson, called *Puppets Party* and *Passport to Limbo*,

27

Housman's *Victoria Regina*, etc., and from then on I knew my work had started in earnest. The standards she had drawn from me would have to be maintained. There was no satisfaction from her until as near perfection as possible had been squeezed, albeit through blood, sweat and tears. Now was born my desire to play the great roles, the comedies could come later, but serious work was from now on my quest. I was beginning to get dissatisfied with being a big frog in a small pond. I wanted to see other artists, great artists at work. I wanted to learn, to be surrounded by challenge. To feel that the roles I was playing were because I had won them in competition and not because there was no one else to play them. England was constantly looming before me, but now the war was raging heavily and everyone laughed at me whenever I mentioned going, and anyway, I hadn't any money to get there.

I had had a particularly gruelling summer at the hands of my new master. I was now in my eighteenth year, and I stopped to take stock of my life to date. Certainly I was a star in my own town. I had sacrificed absolutely all else to achieving just that. I refused the invitations of the young men my own age, and when I did find one I happened to like and invited him home, my eldest sister, who was even more attractive by now and more mature and therefore more interesting to them, whisked them unconsciously from under my nose each time. In the end I lost heart and gave up trying. So I suppose I was ripe to be gathered up into the arms of the first person who would love me the way I wanted to be loved, which was of course nothing short of Héloïse and Abélard or Beatrice and Dante or Antony and Cleopatra. So it was hardly surprising that I was to experience one of those harsh tricks of fate which looking back on it now are I suppose all part of life's maturity machine.

Chapter 3

I DECIDED to take a short rest down in Durban and stayed at the Edward Hotel, which was and still is a large comfortable and amusing place right on the beach. We had been going there for years and consequently became absorbed in a large and congenial family atmosphere. The Indian waiters called me Miss Moira and the owner kept a paternal eye on me. A convoy had come in and belched forth its precious cargo of soldiers, sailors and airmen for the three-week last fling before going into action in the desert.

Being tired and rather depressed, I was not particularly interested in the high festivities that usually accompanied these forays. But as we are such puppets in the hands of destiny whether I was interested or not was pretty unimportant. I was sitting alone one lunchtime in the dining room savouring one of the delicious curries that the Indians make so well and had just filled my plate from the myriad little dishes of various hot chillies, chutneys, peppers, etc., and had popped the first far-too-hot morsel into my mouth, when I looked up and found a pair of deep violet eyes looking at me from the doorway. They belonged to a beautiful young man in a captain's uniform with black undulating hair drawn back from a high brow and framing a face of almost perfect structure. I was so mesmerised I swallowed the chili whole and nearly burnt my epiglottis right off.

He was with five or six other officers, but they were just a khaki blur. As they all passed my table being ushered to theirs, I buried my head in my curry which I now couldn't have eaten if it had been a soufflé made of gossamer. They sat down at the other side of the vast dining room and he sat facing me, and I could feel the intensity of his gaze even from that distance. I toyed with my curry which now looked revolting and stuck in my throat until I could bear it no longer, picked up my bag and made a dignified if somewhat shaky exit into the lounge and ordered coffee. I must have been on about my seventh cup by the time they finished lunch and started to file out of the dining room. My first instinct was to run out and go to my room but lead seemed to have filtered into my legs and feet, so I just sat where I was. They ordered coffee and eventually one of the other officers came over to my table and said, "Graham is longing for you to join us for coffee but hasn't the courage to ask you. So will you accept the invitation from us all?" I looked round at the sea of smiling faces with Graham sinking in a wave of embarrassment in the middle of it. I pulled a rather, "Well-I-really-shouldn't-but-I-will" face and graciously accepted. They all introduced themselves, none of whose names I registered except Mr. Violet Eyes, who was presented as Captain Graham Matthews. Well, from the moment we started to talk to each other, there was a tremendous rapport. We liked the same things, we laughed at the same nonsenses, we had read the same poets. I began to experience an alarming floating feeling. We talked through several more cups of coffee until we realised that one by one the rest of the group had surreptitiously made themselves scarce and that we were alone. Now I panicked and gathered my things together, asking if he would excuse me as I had an appointment I had to keep. He asked when he could see me again, and I said, trying to be nonchalant, that I would probably be on the beach the following morning. I said goodbye and went straight up to my room, locked the door and lay panting on my bed. My head was swimming, my heart thumping and my breath short and sharp. I was completely bewildered. I had never felt like this before. It was ridiculous. I didn't know this man at all. How could he have such a deep effect on me. I tried to pull myself together and be reasonable. I tossed and turned and finally fell into an exhausted sleep and dreamed of a rose-covered cottage in the heart of a picturesque fifteenth-century English village with him sitting at the head of a table on the lawn under the ancient oak and me, pouring tea for him and our six devastating-looking children!

I awoke the next morning rather ashamed of my foolish sentimentality and decided to play the whole thing very cool. I took my swimming things and went on to the beach. I cast furtive glances up and down the golden sands but couldn't see him anywhere. In a way I was relieved but in another not very pleased that I had got there first, lest it appeared I might seem too eager. However, I sunbathed for half an hour, then decided to swim. The water didn't look very appetising as it happened that up-country there had been a great storm and the rivers had flooded and in their frenzied search for their outlet to the sea had gathered more trees and roots and branches than lay in any tropical jungle. However, I was hot and needed to cool off, so ran in and dived under an enormous breaker. As I surfaced simply covered in twigs and leaves and fronds, Graham, who must have dived in at the same moment and who came up equally camouflaged, greeted me with, "Dr. Livingstone, I presume!"

We laughed our way through the rest of the morning, lunched on the beach, then drove in the late afternoon through the swaying sugar-cane fields with the blades of the natives' scythes glistening like pink diamonds in the reflection of the setting sun as they cut through the cane. The melodious harmonising of the native voices complemented our mood like Guinness does champagne.

But clouds, like cloud seven, are transitory, and are apt to disintegrate if one tries to make them tangible. Wanting not to break our mood, I suggested that we go to the nightclub that night and dance till dawn. Here the first little seed of the horror into which I was unsuspectingly plunging was born – and instead of examining it more closely, I chose, through cowardice, to ignore it. His face fell at the suggestion and his reply was, "I have never been to a nightclub." This I could hardly believe; he looked a born dancer, loved music and was, after all, thirty-two years old. I laughed at him and said I didn't believe him. "Why?" I said, "What are you afraid of?" "Nothing," he said. "But don't ask me any more questions, just let's leave it like that." "All right," I said, longing to know, but afraid of the answer. "But you're jolly well coming with me tonight."

At first he was slightly uneasy, but gradually the warmth of my affection broke down his reserves and indeed we danced till dawn and he held me very tightly, in, I couldn't help feeling, a slightly desperate way. However, I chose again not to pry. As the first light of dawn coloured the sky, we drove straight to the beach. We still had our costumes in the car and lay down in the warm early breeze on the virgin sands and dozed for an hour or two, till the Indian waiters started bustling around with trays of luscious tropical fruit salads, orange juice freshly squeezed and crisp hot scones.

So the day meandered on with a wonderful relaxed warmth and understanding as if we had known each other intimately all our lives. Everything seemed to gell, everything was so right, and apart from his occasional evasiveness, it was as near perfect a relationship as I could have dreamed of. That night we drove to the lagoon formed by the mouth of the river opening out into the sea, which was a haven for shark fishermen who had great games fighting to the death to land these monsters who in turn had come in from the sea to gorge the cattle and sheep that had been washed into the river by the floods. It was very exciting to watch and whenever the contest between man and beast became too terrifying I would feel a protective arm go round my shoulders and those violet eyes would smile reassuringly at me.

From there we drove to Umhlanga Rocks to dine at the

32

Oyster Box Hotel. Here as we sat at a table overlooking the sea with huge breakers crashing on the rocks almost at our feet, the oyster pickers literally picked the oysters that we were going to have for our meal. They were a picturesque little group of ten coloured women of mixed races – one or two Indians in their saris, two or three Zulu girls with their bare breasts and their hair coiffured with mud and gaily coloured beads, some half-caste slightly scruffy ones and two native women with their tiny babies tied on their backs in the usual native fashion. There was one man, the head man, an old native who had been doing the job for years. He gave each girl a steel pole with a sharp pick at the end with which to prise the oysters off the rocks. They would then bring each oyster to him, which he in turn put through a metal ring – if the oyster was still small enough to go through the ring, it was thrown back into the sea, but if it got stuck just in the middle of the ring, then it was the perfect size and was allowed to go into the basket which was then brought to the table to be prepared.

I knew Graham was enjoying all this tremendously and more so when he said, "You're taking a terrible risk feeding me with all these oysters!" I had no idea what he meant as my seventeen years had not yet embraced the knowledge of oysters having aphrodisiac qualities. I replied with something witty like, "No risk with you could be a bad risk!" But somewhere sub-consciously there was a tiny suspicion that perhaps I didn't quite believe that. All during dinner I longed to ask him questions about himself but always I was afraid of the answers. However, by the time the coffee arrived, I had determined at least to find out if he was married. I took a deep breath and confronted him with the question. A momentary black look crossed his face, but it quickly changed into a smile. "No, I'm not!" Divorced? "No." Engaged? "No, and that's enough. No more questions, but I tell you what" – and he leaned across and took both my hands in his – "if you promise to be a good girl and not spoil our precious moments, as soon as we get our embarkation orders I will tell you my dark secret." And as I looked into those beautiful eyes, they seemed to become clouded with a despair so deep that it sent a pain shooting down inside me. "All right. All right. I'm sorry." But I had spoiled the atmosphere and the conversation became the empty words of strangers. We were separated by our own worlds through which we had to grapple before we could finally reach each other again.

After dinner he took my hand and we walked under the sweet-smelling frangipani trees. The stars were shining and the moon reflecting on the waters. On a little promontory was a giant boabab tree with its outsize wrinkled trunk and its strange stunted branches, like a Gustave Doré etching. We rested against this drinking in the scene around us. Suddenly he took me in his arms and kissed me deeply. Then he said, "Please remember whatever happens, I love you with every fibre of my being and the guilt is mine alone." Strange as these words were, I almost didn't hear them. All I knew was that my heart and body were almost at bursting point. But stronger was my religious upbringing as a Roman Catholic, and my belief that my entire life would be ruined if I gave myself to any man outside the holy sacrament of marriage. So the fact that he didn't carry me off to bed, I, in my innocence, took as a great mark of respect, and loved him even more!

So the days and nights went by in an idyllic kind of existence. I asked no more questions and lived each moment as though it was the most precious and most rare that I was ever to know. And indeed they probably were. Every day brought us closer. He gave me a book of the poems of Francis Thompson which we read together. He read to me *The Hound of Heaven*. So beautifully that when he got to the end, I suddenly said, "You're a Catholic too, aren't you?" "Yes," he said. "I am."

It was just three weeks since we had met when the dreaded moment came and embarkation orders were given. He came to the hotel very early that morning and said, "This is our last day. We leave tonight. Come quickly, let us go out somewhere where we can be alone."

I grabbed my swimsuit and bag and car keys and we ran to the car and just drove in silence, hardly being able to bear to speak. We got to a little beach just beyond the main beach, and threw ourselves on to the hot golden sands and lay clutched in each other's arms. He clung on to me in a desperate kind of way and I gathered him in my arms almost feeling I had more strength than he – and yet it was a mixture of maternal and immature love. My maturity was to come at the end of the day.

I longed, of course, for him to say something about the future, give me some hope to let me feel that it wasn't all going to end like this. But he said nothing that I could hold on to. So the hours slipped by. We swam, we lay in each other's arms, we kissed and caressed, but all the time I had the nagging pain that I would have to be the one to ask him the burning question of what it was that he was keeping from me.

Finally, about five o'clock in the evening, I braced myself by thinking that whatever it was it couldn't be that bad. So I tried, as calmly as I could, to get a smile on my face and gaily said, "Well, my boy, what are you hiding from me?" He looked at me then, his head dropped and he drew patterns in the sand with a twig. Very gently he said, "I thought you had guessed by now." "No, I certainly haven't and I'll thank you to put me out of my misery." Again he was silent as though trying to ward off the final blow. He said, "I thought of going back to the ship this morning and not seeing you again. It would have been easier that way and you need never have known, but I couldn't throw away our last day. So now I have to face telling you and I'm afraid of your reaction." I began to feel sick and cold. What was this thing? Had he done "time"? Had he been castrated, had he committed a murder? What was this great barrier that stood between us that he found so difficult to tell me about?

35

"Come," I said. "Tell me, I'll try to understand." He said, "I don't think you will understand, but I have to tell you now – I am a practising Roman Catholic priest and have been ordained for the past nine years."

I couldn't speak. I went numb, I kept opening and closing my mouth. No sound came forth and I sat there dumbstruck, swallowing, unable to move. No words formed in my brain. I couldn't think of anything. All I felt was a tremendous pressure on my chest as though I was being forced into the ground. I was conscious that he was talking, but I didn't hear very well what he was saying. Vaguely in the distance I heard words like, "Talk to me – say something – hit me – do something – don't just sit there staring."

I tried to speak – nothing – just the pain in my chest. I don't know how long I sat like that, but the next thing I knew I was walking towards the sea. Water, I thought, water, that'll ease the pain. I walked through the waves and then started to swim out to sea. The waves were huge, the currents dangerous. I am a strong swimmer but I swam slowly with long strokes. I swam out and out and gradually I started thinking – here is peace – no one can hurt me here, the pain is easier in my chest – go on, swim further, the further you swim the safer you are, there's peace here, no one can touch you, swim further – deeper, deeper. Gradually water was covering my head, my body was getting heavier, but still I was only aware that here was peace, no one could touch me here. I opened my eyes and saw that I was under the water completely now. I had no desire to fight back up. I closed my eyes and lost consciousness.

The next sensation was of pain again. This time the pressure was on my back. I was confused. I was being sick. Water was pouring from my mouth – a life-saver, I realised, was giving me artificial respiration. Each time he bore down on me, I dug my fingers in the sand. Don't revive me, I thought, let me die. But I still couldn't mouth the words. I just lay there, passively. Then I became aware of Graham's voice saying, "Is she all right, is

36

she breathing, will she die?" He was reassured that I was out of danger. Graham begged the life-saver to let him take me back to the hotel himself if I was fit enough. With a few instructions as to what to do for me, he was allowed to take me. He gathered me in his arms and carried me to the car. It was now six-thirty and his embarkation was at eight p.m. He put me in the car and drove at breakneck speed to the hotel. I just lay on the car seat. He talked incessantly, begging forgiveness, chastising me for trying to take my life, trying to put his case, to explain his reasons: that he'd never wanted to be a priest, that it was his mother who had forced it on him, but now that he was, and the war was on, and he was needed at the front, etc., etc., etc. I caught snatches of what he was saying, but I kept lapsing into a comatose state for several minutes at a time.

We arrived at the hotel, and with his help and not wanting anyone to know what had happened I summoned all my strength to walk on his arm into the hotel and get my key and allow him to help me to my room. He took my clothes off and put me into my bed. Then knelt beside me and cradled me in his arms. He was distraught, he cried, he begged all through the ghastly silence which I didn't seem able to break. What seemed to worry him most was that he may have caused me to lose my faith. He implored me to keep that – that he wasn't representative of the church, that he was one weakling among millions who were strong and worthy, that one day I would laugh at him and at myself and that if I was a Christian, forgiveness was one of the first things I had to learn.

All through this descant I lay staring at the ceiling unable to make one cogent remark, until the final moment came when he had to leave me and walk out of my life for ever. He took my head between his hands and put his lips on mine. Mine were cold and unrewarding. His were warm and pleading. "Please, before I go, just say in time you will forgive." I tried but couldn't. I took his hand and put it to my cheek and held it there a moment, then buried my face in the pillow and waved to him to go. I heard the door close and knew I would never hear from him again.

In fact, many years later, under very different circumstances, I did meet him again, but that I will come to in the appropriate time in my life.

I lay in that bed for three days and three nights. He had had the grace to inform the hotel doctor what had happened and told him to look after me. At the end of the third day, the doctor phoned my mother, who drove the five hundred miles from Johannesburg and took me home.

But as is said, "'Tis an ill wind", and maybe that was the shock that I needed to spur me to move my life and career to broader horizons.

Chapter 4

AFTER a few weeks at home in Johannesburg in the loving tender care of my wonderful mother, I gradually came out of my torpor and started to live a little again. But it was a very different me. My ideals had been shattered, my religious beliefs shaken to their foundations and the givingness and warmth of my nature turned inside out. I became introvert and cold and untrusting, particularly where men were concerned. I trusted none of them and vowed never to give my affections again. I would stick to my dream world of the theatre and strictly avoid the world of reality with which I felt illequipped to cope.

So I threw myself headlong into my work. Radio, plays, producing, writing, always determined to get back to England. Leontine Sagan, my Svengali, was naturally delighted to see the intensity with which I attacked my work. It became all-embracing and absorbed me completely.

My two sisters seemed to be managing their lives far better. Doreen was now married and was the proud mother of a beautiful boy. And Evelyn had sold her piano and received permission from Pretoria, as the war was still on, to take a one-way passage to India to marry an officer of a Gurkha regiment whom she had met on a happier convoy than mine.

My desire to get to England now became obsessive. I thought about it all the time. I started collecting and making clothes for my trip. Everyone laughed at me for even thinking of going. My eldest sister accused me of potentially being responsible for my mother's death because she would never get over it if anything happened to me. But of course the major problem was getting the money to make the trip. I discovered that to go on a troop-ship with several thousand other passengers only cost thirty nine pounds – but then I had to get to Cape Town, a thousand miles away, and live there until a boat came in. I would have to have a little capital to keep me in England before I could get a job. Much as I wanted to go, I had too much pride to ask my poor father to foot the bill again and anyway, he simply scoffed at the idea, keeping all cuttings for me of every sinking in the Atlantic of which there were a great number – all the horror stories of the survivors and the deaths at sea of exposure, thirst, sharks, etc. He gave them all to me almost every day. I tried terribly hard to save the few pennies I earned, but there were always the day to day contingencies that had to be catered for and, as always, at the end of the month I was skint.

However, in March of 1943, the fates decided it was time to stop me boring the pants off everyone and call my bluff. It was near the end of the month and I had three pounds left in the kitty. My eldest sister invited me to the Johannesburg Races. I jumped at the chance. Was this to be my lucky day? I put a pound on the first race and lost, a pound on the second race and lost. The next two races constituted the double. I had one pound left. I asked a man standing next to me what would win the double. He shrugged his shoulders and said, "Number three and number nine." "Thank you," I said and went on my way to buy the tickets. My sister tried to stop me. "You're mad," she said. "He's only telling you that to get rid of you. At least ask someone who knows something." "Well, who knows anything," I said. "If I'm meant to win, I'll win. If not – I won't." I bought number three and number nine for a pound. The next race number three romped home, but the second race was tougher. Number nine was fighting all the way against a nebulous number one. And from where I stood it looked like number one had won. I was just about to tear up my ticket when a photo-finish was announced. I held my breath for the full developing time of that little picture, saying countless Hail Mary's at the same time. And lo and behold, number nine won by a nose. I had pulled off the double. Then there was the hiatus while they worked out how much they would pay. My mind was spinning. Whatever it was, it must be enough to pay my fare. Plans were forming and falling over themselves. My whole future life seemed to tumble out in those few moments. At last the decision was made, the board went up and on it, was written one hundred and twenty pounds for one pound. I was delirious. I jumped, I danced, I screamed for joy. I rushed to the pay-box and was there first with trembling hands to hold more pound-notes than I had ever seen together at one time.

I gathered my sister and we rushed home. But I couldn't resist making the most of the moment and playing a joke on my parents. I went into the drawing room with a very long face and told my father I had done a terrible thing in borrowing twenty pounds from a friend at the races. As I had lost it, would he pay my debt for me. He hit the roof. Screamed at me for being irresponsible, dishonest, borrowing money I couldn't repay, etc., etc. I could see on my poor mother's face that she was already deciding that she was going to have to pay for me. And indeed my father, determining to teach me a lesson, refused to pay. I rose to my feet from my cowed position and with great panache and gesture said: "Right, you refuse to pay for me – very well, I will pay it myself." And I opened my handbag and threw all the notes up into the air, so that they floated down like manna from heaven. Great relief all round. Mother cried. Father embarrassed, said something that was to turn out very true, alas. He said, "I'm very sorry you have won this money so easily because you will give it back again and again." And indeed I have. I love gambling, but I'll never make any fortune that way. And because I realise that I am on the whole unlucky, I don't take too many chances. But just at that moment, the doors of the world became opened to me and in a gust of confidence and expectation, I flew through them.

Now followed all the delaying details that had to be tied up before I could go. First I had to get a permit to leave the country. How was I to do this – they would laugh at me in Pretoria if I said I wanted to cross the Atlantic in face of bloody battle, to go to England to go on the stage. So I had to think of something else.

Then I remembered Evelyn having got a permit to go to India to get married. "Ah," I thought, "why can't I go to England to get married?" All I needed was a fiancé in England, quite easy for someone with my wild imagination. Of course I knew no one there who would be remotely suitable, but had I not met the year before that nice Major Spencer who had so politely said, "If ever you are in England, do look me up?" Well, I knew he was safely or unsafely in the Middle East somewhere, fighting for his country and his life, so he would be singularly unobtainable and would never know that I had used his name and address as my betrothed. So, filled with a huge confidence I wrote off to Pretoria giving his name, saying that I intended to marry him and required a permit to go to England so to do. Incredibly my audacity paid off and within two weeks my permit came through. I was out of my mind with joy. This was now the moment of truth, there was nothing to stop me. I had the fare, I had the permit and I had an overwhelming desire to go. But, but, but . . . first and foremost there was the war which was raging at its full and most formidable height right in the Atlantic which I would have to cross, there was England struggling for survival against insuperable odds, the unmanned missiles were just beginning, doodle-bugs and V2s pouring over the channel and blasting hell out of English town and country, and there were enormous casualties from sinkings off and around the Cape. Then there were the closer-to-home obstacles, like my father who was dead against the whole ridiculous project; my sister, who threatened me with having my mother's life on my conscience for the rest of my life; and then there was my beloved mother herself. She was the one who really disturbed me. I looked at her brave little face so many times during those preparatory days and always she was encouraging and smiling, but I knew behind it all she was simply choking. At last I could bear it no more and faced her with it. "Mummy," I said. "We must be honest with each other. I know what you are going through and I want you to tell me the truth. If you were my age, with whatever gifts and talents God may have given me and you were placed in a similar position, and you were faced with the decision, what would you do?" She looked deeply at me and said, "It breaks my heart to tell you this, but I must. If I were in your shoes I would go. And one day if you have the luck to play Shakespeare and you come across the lines 'There is a tide in the affairs of men which taken at the flood leads on to victory', just remember me!"

So that was it. My mind was irrevocably made up and I booked my seat on the train from Johannesburg to take the one-thousand-mile journey alone to the Cape, the first leg of my voyage. All my friends rallied round with wonderful presents of all the things I would not be able to get in England. Stockings, undies, clothes, costume jewellery, until my two trunks swelled with goodies. Then they all came to the station to give me the big send off: "Moira Lister goes to London to find fame and fortune." I didn't tell them, of course, my dark secret of how I had perjured myself to get the permit. My two best friends had had leis of frangipani flowers made and as I leaned out of the carriage window they put them round my neck. Everyone was in tears of course and so I was greatly relieved when the train finally chuffed out of the station and with my little host of family and friends, my last link with security grew lilliputian in the distance. I wondered whether I would ever see any of them again. I sat back in the compartment and breathed in the sweet pungent smell of the frangipani.

I closed my eyes and was too numbed to indulge in any cogent thoughts. I just sat there and let the train cradle me in its rhythmic rocking to my destination.

Towards evening as we were passing through the Karoo, that vast parched desert of scrub where the sunsets are so crimson that they seem to mirror the deep red earth and join together with it, making a huge and flaming furnace on the horizon, we stopped at a siding. There was one solitary little pool of water from the well dug on the side of the track to cool the engine. I got down from the train and placed my frangipani on the water and left them there so that I would not see them die.

Next morning through the splendour of the Drakensberg and into Cape Town, with majestic Table Mountain nestling under her tablecloth of white cloud, flanked by Devils Peak and Lions Head. The train pulled into the station and I realised almost for the first time that here I was, alone, eighteen, in Cape Town, en route for England, but that I had no boat ticket, no passage booked, nowhere to sleep that night, a hundred pounds in my pocket and two trunks at my feet.

The challenge galvanised me into action. I deposited my trunks and tried one or two hotels, all far too expensive. Finally I came down to one little room which I reckoned I could suffer for the few hours until my boat left. Little did I know how those few hours were going to stretch and stretch. However, oblivious as I was, I marched buoyantly from there to the biggest shipping company. I said I wanted to buy a ticket on the very next boat, leaving from Cape Town for England, no matter what kind of boat, but I must leave immediately. Good-naturedly humouring me, the man asked me to sit down and explain to him my case. This I did with great rapidity, showed him proudly my permit to go to England to marry my unwitting Major and explaining that once I had paid the passage, there would be very little left to live on out of my hundred pounds and that I must keep some to live on in

44

England until the wedding. I didn't bother to enlighten him that in my mind the wedding meant the vows I was going to take to love, honour and obey the theatre. "My dear young lady," he said sympathetically, as one would to a wildly insane child, "I must point out that no passenger has been allowed to leave these shores for the past three months and that refugees from North Africa and survivors from passing ships have been accumulating in vast numbers on high priorities waiting to get out. Of course eventually they will be allowed to go when proper warships and destroyers can be spared from the battle raging in the Atlantic to convey them, but how long that will be is impossible to predict."

I was desolate. "What can I do?" I said.

"Nothing, absolutely nothing but sit like all the others and wait."

"Will you put me on the list and take my money for the passage?"

"Well, if that will make you feel any better, I will. But it doesn't guarantee anything at all."

So down my name went with thousands of other passengers and my fare, which he promised to refund if I didn't use it, was at least paid. That left me with sixty-one pounds and an indefinite time during which to eke it out. I went back to my little room and cried with disappointment, but through my tears I counted out twenty one-pound notes and put them in an envelope and marked it "London". That at all costs I must keep to live on once I got there. That left forty-one pounds. I counted those forty-one notes several times, and finally decided that as I was feeling so depressed I needed cheering up. I put the forty pounds under the mattress and took the one pound and marched determinedly to the nearest restaurant and ordered crayfish (they were only one and six each) and a bottle of cheap wine and enjoyed the meal knowing I was to be thrown to the lions the next morning, by having to find a means of livelihood to finance my waiting period.

I got up early next morning with a splitting headache from the raw wine I had drunk the night before, but went out to buy the morning paper to look in the "situations vacant" column. But as always my life seems to be pushed by some mystic force. I was walking along the main street in Cape Town, when I bumped into a man whom I'd met two or three times in Johannesburg who was sort of on the fringe of theatre and was always dabbling in various show-business ventures. I had a slight suspicion that it was really the dolly ladies he was after more than the artistic fulfilment, but as he was now rising sixty I assumed he had got things in their right perspective. However, when he asked me to have a cup of coffee with him I readily accepted, mentally adding up how many Danish pastries I could consume in the time. While we were having coffee he asked me what I was doing and I briefly explained my situation, saying that I would be very interested in finding a temporary job. His eyes lit up like neon lights and he explained that he was just embarking on a venture in which I would be an invaluable help.

He was organising a big country fair in one of the outlying country towns sponsored by the very rich farmers. Apart from the usual fun-fair side-shows he had the unique idea of having a small tent in which he could offer a short performance of, say, forty minutes twice nightly, coupled with drinks from a bar and refreshment if required, and to dress in old Voortrekker style with a small band playing Afrikaans folk music. He asked if I could work out a forty-minute act that would amuse the farmers and their wives.

This was a tall order as I had never done anything like it before – but desperate for work I said, "Of course I could," given a few days to work it up and then do it for him to see if it was any good. He said he couldn't afford to pay much but if I would accept ten pounds for the week that would include rehearsal time, etc.

I accepted gladly and went home and set about digging

through my trunks to find suitable material. I worked out a kind of song and dance routine with a couple of impersonation monologues and finishing with a rousing Afrikaans ditty. I rehearsed with the little three-piece band, then showed him my efforts. He was very pleased and said I was engaged. So on the appointed first day of the Fair I drove out the fifty miles to the fairground with the band and he had done an excellent job. It was very gay, if a little like a circus, but had all the requisite trimmings for a week's fun for the entertainment-starved farmers for miles around. My little tent was very nicely equipped with a tiny stage and my name painted on the side of the tent in a poster-like frame. I was delighted and got down to work full of enthusiasm. The audience seemed to like the show, although in my heart I think I admitted to myself that it was more a question of taking the weight off their feet and having a drink that pulled them in and not the splendour of my performance. However, I didn't really mind, I kept thinking of the ten pounds that was going to be mine at the end of the week. One or two of the farmers did leave a tip for me with the barman, which I readily accepted!

It was after the fourth night that everything took an unfortunate – to say the least – turn. After the show my friend invited me out to dinner in Cape Town. So after the show we went to his car and I asked where we were going.

"Well, as I rather fancy myself as a cook, I thought I'd do you something special at my flat."

I was naturally disappointed as I had mentally decided to go through the entire menu and stoke up for the week. However, I thought he'd probably make something nice, so I said, "That would be lovely."

We arrived at a modern block. It was a beautiful position overlooking the sea, but was soon to become a nightmare to me. However, oblivious as a newborn fly, I walked into my spider's web, which glistened brightly and looked very inviting. I took off my coat and he offered me a drink. I hardly

47

drank anything in those days, but trying to be sophisticated, I accepted a small gin and tonic. We stood on the balcony and drank our drinks, chatting of inconsequentials. He insisted I have another drink and when I was about halfway through, he put his arm round my shoulders. This I took as a kind of fatherly affection and I smiled up at him almost gratefully, but when I looked into his face, his expression was anything but fatherly. I tried to tell myself this was sheer imagination, by which time he was leading me to a large divan in his drawing room. "Why don't you put your feet up here while I get the food. Come, let me take your shoes off. That's it, put your feet up."

I allowed myself to be guided by him because I simply couldn't believe that he could have any ulterior motive and yet, at the same time, my heart was beginning to thump with fear. Then to my horror he came to lie next to me. He was a huge man, singularly unattractive and probably three times my age. Still trying not to appear unsophisticated I said, "What about that lovely meal you were going to make?"

"That will come," he said, "after we've had our little aperitif," and with that, his great bulk rolled on to me and his mouth was covering my face with a drool of lecherous kisses. I felt sick and disgusted and revolted, and at the same time very frightened. I started to struggle, but the more I fought the more he pushed me down.

"You're being ridiculous," I said. "If you don't stop I shall scream very loud."

He laughed in my face. "Go ahead, scream. Who do you think will take any notice. You came here of your own accord, no one forced you. I shall simply say that like all actresses you're neurotic and scream easily. But as far as I am concerned, I brought you here for my pleasure, and my pleasure is what I am going to have. So you'd better be quiet." Upon which he started to tear my clothes from me.

How was I going to get out of this? Certainly not by strength

48

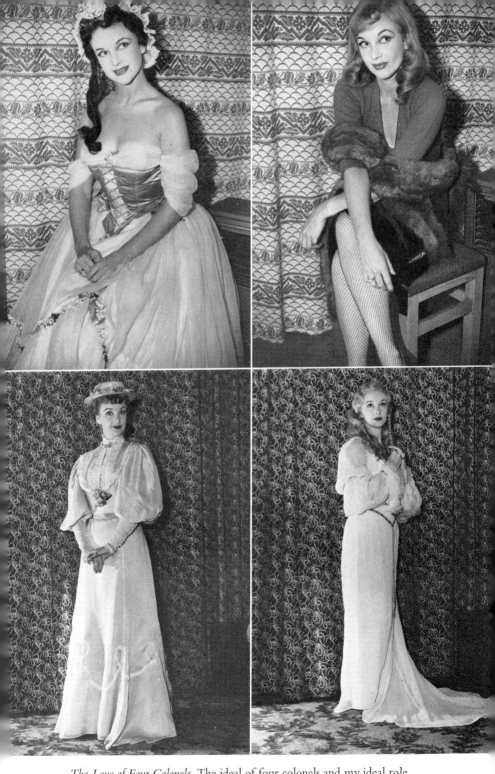

The Love of Four Colonels. The ideal of four colonels and my ideal role

Peter Ustinov, father and creator of the four colonels

Douglas Fairbanks, a real colonel and a dish!

– he was like a bull in full charge. Wildly my brain started clicking. I remembered there was a bathroom next to the front door. If I could only get there I might have a chance of escape. So, with a jerk of my head, I freed my face from his and said, "All right, I was only being silly. Of course you can make love to me, but let's do it properly, let me go and take my clothes off and prepare myself for you and then we can enjoy it." It was a desperate chance I took, but it paid off. He released me and said, "All right, but hurry."

So, trying to be calm and not move too fast to give myself away, I took my handbag and went into the bathroom and locked the door. By the grace of God there was a small fanlight window out of the bathroom on to the outside landing. I squeezed my head out of it as stealthily as I could, the rest of my body following like a coil of rope. I unwound myself, dropped down on to my hands and crept past his front door, tore down the steps and rushed out into the black night. This part was almost worse than the previous scene. I could see absolutely nothing. I soon knew I was on the edge of a cliff, and I could hear the sea crashing on the rocks several hundred feet below, and I knew that any minute he would discover I had gone and start chasing me.

So blindly I stumbled on, clutching at rocks, grasping stumps of bushes, my hands and legs bleeding, terrified I was going to make a false step and hurtle to my death below. It seemed an interminable time before I dared stop even to listen for footsteps behind me. But eventually I was so out of breath and my heart was beating so fast, I had to stop and know the worst. No, there was no sound except the sea below. So, after I had rested a while, I tried to take stock of where I was. I had no idea. Then in the far distance I saw a light, so I made towards it, to discover it was a tiny house and the light was coming from an upstairs room. I had to find out where the nearest hotel was, so I rang the bell. Eventually the door opened and an absolute gargoyle of a face appeared, huge, bloated red lips, swollen red protruding eyes and pock-marked flesh surrounding it all. I can still see every detail of it to this day. And before I could even ask my question, he slammed the door in my face. I turned and fled terrified that he might decide to follow me. Fortunately his house was at the end of a sort of dirt road and I was able to follow it until I came to more houses and eventually I came across a little hotel and rang the bell. It was by now about three a.m. and a very sleepy little Irish porter came to the door. He was about to turn me away when he realised I was a rather pitiable sight and so took compassion on me and allowed me in. He didn't ask any questions but showed me to a little clean room and a few minutes later brought me a cup of tea. I drank it down and sobbed myself to sleep in the pillow.

Now I was faced with an intolerable situation. I still had four more nights to perform but to do this it meant contact with this man. I was terrified of his reaction – he had seemed so violent. He might easily beat me up. Yet, I was billed on my little tent and there was my ten pounds. So I just had to go. Screwing up my courage I went to the usual meeting place where the boys of the band picked me up, praying he would not be there, and mercifully he was not.

He had left, presumably, in his own car earlier in the day. I got in with the boys and didn't breathe a word to them about what had happened. I arrived at the fairground and went over to my tent and lifted the flap. There he was sitting at the table on the empty stage waiting for me with the wrath of God written all over his face. I took a deep breath and decided to pretend nothing had happened. I tried to walk past him with dignity to get to my dressing room but he had other ideas. He grabbed my arm in a vice-like grip. "What the hell game do you think you are playing, you little bitch. I spent half the night looking for you." My heart missed a beat at the thought of him out there on those cliffs, chasing me. "Now I will show you who calls the tune here – you clear your muck out of the dressing room and be out of this tent in ten minutes." With an almighty shove, he threw me on the floor at his feet. As I was trying to get up, he gave me a last vicious kick and said, "Hurry up about it."

When I walked out of the tent with my little bag he had gone, but not without pasting a large card right across my name on the bill-poster which simply read "Cancelled". As I walked disconsolately away towards the railway station, I wondered how many people at the fair would give even a passing thought to what lay behind that one word "Cancelled".

Chapter 5

THERE was still no sign of a boat so I went to stay for a few days on a farm in Somerset West. It was a superb Cape Dutch house and the old slave quarters had been converted into a modern kind of studio den for the teenage children. What a wonderful life they lead. Up at sunrise, on to the horses and ride wild along the mountains, through acres of arum lilies, then up through the protea plantations with their myriad colours making a sort of Aladdin's carpet swaying in the cool morning air. Down again to a large breakfast of great bunches of freshly picked grapes, peaches with the dew still on them, bowls of steaming mealie meal, a sort of refined oatmeal porridge with thick cream and sugar; home-made marmalade with fat chunks of orange that really tasted as if they had been picked the day before. Fresh eggs still warm from the chick and the most gorgeous wholemeal home-made bread. All of course served by shining black native boys clad in shining white suits with red sashes.

The morning was spent either fishing in the mountain rivers, doing the rounds of the farm, playing tennis or just dozing in the sun. Lunch was simply an entire lamb spit-roast in the garden with all the most delicious salads and appendages possible. Everyone ate and drank copiously and then fell asleep in the afternoon. It was all easy, relaxed and in fact there for the asking. The young man of the house seemed all prepared to make the necessary advances had I given the slightest encouragement, but I found myself evaluating the kind of life on which I was about to embark with all its uncertainties, its heights, its depths, its insecurity, its fascination, its continual challenges plus all its sidekicks such as I had just experienced, and comparing it with a life of complete solidity, a superb background in which to bring up a host of children, protection, warmth, love, all the things I suppose one could ask of life. And yet, there was never any question in my mind which of the two I wanted. So off I trundled back to my little dark room in Cape Town.

By now two months had gone by and my money was getting extremely short. So I accepted the invitation of some friends to stay with them in a little house out in the Cape flats.

It was a modest little house, but I had a nice room and they were terribly kind to me. I was able to study undisturbed and in exchange for sitting in with their one-year-old baby when they wanted to go out, I had all the necessary comforts. But as it happened, it turned out to be a sorry move for me.

They employed a little Cape coloured maid, who looked about sixteen, very pretty and very sharp. She travelled in every day from a place called Tiger Valley which was a large area of sand dunes and tin shacks and bush, in which lived a vast number of mixed coloured races. One day she didn't turn up to work. This is quite usual among the servants as they are not endowed with an over abundance of conscience. So no one paid much attention until I happened to go to my trunk to get something and to my dismay I found it half empty. All the things I had been storing jealously, stockings, undies, dresses, shoes – all gone. This was a bitter blow as I had no money left to spend on replacements and I knew my hosts couldn't afford it either. My blood was up and I was determined to find her. My friends, who were naturally terribly upset, simply said, "Impossible, all we know is that she lives in Tiger Valley and looking for anyone there is like looking for a needle in a haystack, that is providing you could get anyone to set foot in the place for you. It is a hive of crime and vice and extremely dangerous." So I went straight to the police.

"Forget it, miss, we won't go into Tiger Valley and get our

throats cut to retrieve a few bits of clothing. All we can tell you is that there is a Chinaman who runs the only store on the edge of the Valley, he may know the girl. But we advise you not to go."

That was enough for me. I went back home and I dug into my make-up box and found my grease-paint and proceeded to put on my best mulatto make-up. I dressed in the shabbiest clothes I could find, put a scarf on my head to hide my blonde hair, painted a black hair line, wore a pair of glasses so my blue eyes wouldn't be quite so obvious, and off I set for Tiger Valley, furious and determined.

I arrived at the Chinaman's shop on the edge of this black Valley just at sunset; I thought I would be less remarkable at that time. It was a corrugated hut comprising two rooms. One was the shop and one was the bedroom, the door of which was open. I peered in and found two beds, one single one for him and his wife and one double one for his eleven children, the smallest of which were already huddled in it like a litter of puppies. But in one corner stood an enormous white refrigerator, unconnected as there was no electricity in the Valley, but in full use just the same. And in the other corner a large radiogram. This was battery-run and was pouring forth strange Chinese incantations which gave the whole place a very eerie and eastern atmosphere.

I hung around outside the door, mingling with the other coloureds trying to make myself inconspicuous and getting their accents well in my ears before I attempted mine. Eventually I summoned enough courage to go in. I shuffled up to the Chinaman and using my best Cape coloured accent, asked if he knew Sarah van der Merwe.

"Why you want to know?"

"Because I have money for her."

He beckoned me into the corner behind a kind of dangling Chinese screen. "She owe me money. You give me half money and I send my boy with you to her place."

Happily I had brought two of my precious pounds with me, so I gladly gave him one and with a malicious smile he called his fifteen-year-old son to guide me to Sarah's shack. Fortunately the moon was full and very bright, for there were no roads or numbers, simply tin shacks scattered in among the white sand dunes. We crept behind them and jumped from one bush to another, sometimes crawling on our tummies along the sand so as to remain unseen for as long as possible so that no one could run ahead and warn her we were coming. Strange noises came out of the different shacks as we passed unseen. Drunken husbands beating up equally drunken wives, children yelling, hungry dogs whining, and hitting higher notes than the dogs were the crickets heralding the sultry heat under which sweaty bodies gave noise and vent to their sexual gavorts. After about half an hour he stopped behind a little shack and pointed to its door round the other side. "I wait here, me no go in!" So alone I crept to the door. Took a deep breath and pushed the door open as quietly as possible and closed it again behind me.

"Stay where you are," I hissed, "the police are surrounding the house." I could hardly see but I heard shuffling on a mattress on the floor in the far corner. Gradually my eyes became accustomed to the dim light and a scene of unbelievable squalor unveiled itself, to say nothing of the nauseating stench. Pots of porridge, plates of left-overs of some evil smelling food. Bottles of kaffir-beer turned over and half spilt on the floor, a cat finishing off a dead rat and in among all this, everywhere I looked were my clothes. She had obviously been entertaining her lover with a parade of my precious wardrobe. And the crowning injury of all was not only Madame Sarah in her flea-ridden filthy bed wearing my best pink lace nightie but also a huge big buck native lying next to her with not one but several pieces of my undies decked on his various parts like the frilling on a barbecued ox.

They had obviously been surprised by me and huddled motionless in their corner. And I stood equally immobile and sickened in mine. I knew that I would never be able to put my things on me again after their battering, so before I actually vomited, I turned and fled.

The two months slid into three and my spirits were just about as low as they could be. I had moved again to some other friends, and on making my abortive daily visit to the shipping company I was informed that my permit to go to England had expired, as it was only valid for three months. This didn't worry me much. I was sure that as they had granted me one permit it was only a matter of prolonging it for a further period until the boat arrived. I wrote to Pretoria asking for an extension and to my horror they wrote back by return saying that during the last three months conditions had been revised and that I would now have to have a signed affidavit from my fiancé in England confirming he was going to marry me. I was destroyed! I had no fiancé in England. The man whose name I had used was unaware that I had used it in perjury to get the permit, so that I could never ever fulfil this requirement of the Ministry. I went back to my room and paced around like a caged tiger. I couldn't have come so far to be defeated now. I couldn't return to Johannesburg with my tail between my legs saying I had been ignominiously sent back for telling a great fat lie. So, in desperation, I decided the only thing to do was to play for time. Next morning, in order to play the scene convincingly, I went to Woolworth's and bought myself not one, but two three-stone diamond rings for a shilling each (if you're going to dream – dream big!) put them on my third finger and marched to the office of the Minister of Interior. He asked me to what he owed the honour of my visit. I explained that I was engaged to Major Spencer, waving my hand about at a reasonable distance so he couldn't see my diamonds were not all they might appear, and that I was quite prepared to get an affidavit from him in England to say he was going to marry me, but that with the uncertain conditions in the Atlantic today, how did we know how long a letter would take to arrive, if indeed it ever did. And what would happen if a boat came in in the meanwhile?

He looked at me quizzically, "How long have you been engaged?"

"Six months," I said, picking a figure out of the air.

"And how long since you have seen your fiancé?"

"One year—" which was true.

"So he proposed by letter?"

"Yes," I said, having no alternative.

"Right," he said. "Show me the letter."

Thinking very quickly, I countered, "I'm afraid that as I was coming on this trip I only took the absolute minimum with me. Consequently I burnt all my letters before I left Johannesburg."

The ball was now in his court. "I see," he said. "Is there anyone in the country who knows you are going to England to marry Major Spencer?"

"Yes," I said, too quickly and not expecting his next remark. "My father."

"Very well," he said. "Get him to sign the affidavit."

"All right," I said and I walked out of his office, knowing I couldn't ask my father who was a Major in the army to sign a false affidavit. I was quite prepared to sign one myself and take the consequences, but I couldn't possibly ask him. So again I went back to my room defeated and dejected. The end had come. I rang up the family and told them. I had lost and I would have to return. They, of course, said it was a sign from God, my life had been probably saved and one mustn't force one's hand, etc., etc.

All night I tossed and turned, sick with frustration and futility. But at five o'clock in the morning I leapt out of bed with a streak of inspiration. What if I went to the Minister and told him the truth. I had nothing to lose now, and still everything to gain. I couldn't wait till eight-thirty and I was at his door when he arrived. This time without the diamond rings, but armed with my press-cutting book!

"That was quick," he said as he opened the door. "Where's the affidavit?"

"Now wait a minute," I said, "I'm going to come clean and tell you the whole story. I have told a terrible lie. I am not engaged to Major Spencer – he's in the Middle East and hardly knows me. I only made up the story in order to get a permit to leave South Africa and go to London to go on the stage and I was convinced if I told you the truth you would never have given me a permit. But here is my press book to prove at least that I really am an actress and I'm desperate to go."

He looked searchingly at me, trying to decide whether this was another whopper or not. But I detected a slight smile on his face.

"Well," he said, "I think you are raving mad but at least you've got guts. I will give you an extension for two weeks. If a boat comes in during that time you may go to England, but if not, your case will be null and void and you will go back to Johannesburg."

I was so elated I jumped up and thanked him, saying, "When you come to England I will give you seats for any play I am in." As he handed me the permit, he said, "And one evening as well?"

"You can have six," I said grabbing the permit and running to the door, from where I blew him a kiss and disappeared. To date he has never turned up to claim my offer.

Three days later a boat came in.

Chapter 6

Now suddenly all the conjecture, all the soul-searching and questioning disappeared and there was stark reality. Me on the docks looking up at a vast trans-atlantic liner, very unglamorous in its battleship grey. There were no streamers this time, no band playing on the quay, just hundreds of tense and frightened-looking people whose moment had come to leave the beauty of Cape Town's shore and plunge into the unknown, submarine-infested waters. Suddenly I saw a column of three thousand bedraggled, shaven-headed men, each with a plum-coloured bundle under his arm. They were flanked on either side by soldiers with bayonets at the ready. It was a strange sight because the men looked so defeated, the guns seemed so unnecessary. However, I suppose it was necessary as they were three thousand Italian prisoners who for some strange reason were being shipped to England. I never discovered why. The bundle they carried was their prisoner-of-war uniform but they were not allowed to wear it till we got to England. So the empty swimming pool, which not long before had besported the golden bodies of the idle cruising rich, was now a container for three thousand bundles of prisoner's clothing, while the prisoners themselves were herded into the hold where they slept either on the floor or in hammocks.

I had not yet gone on board because I knew that once I put my foot on the gangplank there was no turning back and for the first time I was beginning to wonder whether I should turn heel and run. Then I watched them bringing the wounded on board. Stretcher cases. There must have been very special reasons why they were allowed to do the trip. Then the women and children, refugees from Poland and Egypt, and a handful of civilians and a great many uniformed men of all sorts of mixed denominations. Everyone was very concentrated on getting themselves and their belongings on board. And I was standing somewhat lost in the midst of all the turmoil. I looked round and saw beautiful Table Mountain rising clear and majestic behind Cape Town with its plateau, a sharp clean line against the blue May sky. How many times I had climbed it and was exhilarated by the challenge, but here was a new mountain and a new challenge. Was I going to reach the smooth plateau at the top, I wondered? With a deep breath I gathered my worldly capital – two suitcases – round me, plus the well-clutched envelope containing twenty pounds marked "London" and marched firmly up the gangway. I had scarcely reached the top when a very efficient duty officer said, "All that must go down to the baggage room. No place in the cabins. Take out a pair of slacks, change of underwear, jersey and blouse – that must last you for the trip." As I struggled to undo the zip of my case, two nuns came up the gangway and to my astonishment I heard him repeating the same instructions to them. They were horrified and explained they had no trousers.

"We will issue you with some. It is for your own safety and that of the other passengers. If we are hit and have to abandon ship, you may cause your own death and other passengers' by climbing down rope ladders in that attire and you wouldn't stand a chance in the water with all those heavy clothes."

So the two little nuns were ushered away and I never saw them again, but I heard years later that the taste of the pair of pants and with it liberty and freedom was too much for one of them and she consequently left the orders.

I took my clothes ration under my arm as I watched the rest of my belongings being whisked away. I did manage to sneak my volume of Shakespeare under my clothes.

I looked on the notice-board. There was my name, in an

inside cabin. Claustrophobia in the tropics, I thought. However, I went down wondering who my cabin mate was going to be as it was a two-berth cabin. When I arrived at the door of the cabin there seemed to be an awful lot of people milling in and out of it. To my horror I discovered there were going to be *six* of us in this tiny inside cabin. Shelf bunks had been installed and as I was the youngest of an apparently very decrepit bunch, I was given the top bunk. Underneath me a frail old lady, and at the bottom a really vast woman who insisted on the lower bunk because she had some liver complaint and she never knew "when she was going to be took bad." And when she "took bad", she was very very bad. And indeed, several nights during the voyage the poor thing was taken bad. I have never heard such screams of pain. However, we worked out a rota of dressing and washing, as only two people could stand up at a time in the cabin. But I was so immersed in my dreams coming true that I hardly noticed this sordid side of things and even today the faces of those five other women are completely blurred – I have no idea what any of them looked like.

We seemed to glide out of Cape Town harbour without my even noticing, although we were a large convoy of two civilian ships and various destroyers and battleships. I think we were eight in all. But they were a very comforting sight stretched out in front, behind and at our sides. These large grey bulwarks of strength and strategy. Soon the routine of ship life took over and the six thousand people crammed on a boat which usually held fifteen hundred, seemed to settle down to an extraordinary existence. I think probably I learnt more about people during those three weeks than ever before or since. There was naturally a great tension underlying the apparent calm. But it was not long out of Cape Town that the submarines started to come after us – then the depth charges from our destroyers would go off – rocking the ship with a sickening repercussion. This had different reactions on different people. One refugee woman with eleven children kept putting her latest born in a suitcase out of which she had cut a hole for it to breathe. She felt she could carry it in an emergency more easily. The Polish community seemed to be the most sensitive because of what they had already been through. There were children of twelve to fourteen who looked like women of forty-five. Deep lines of suffering marked their little faces and their eyes seemed dull and glazed. A small band of Italian women decided to take full advantage of the "live for the moment" feeling among the soldiers and started a brothel down in the hold. I can still see the little "Madame" very vividly. She was indescribably unappetising – filthy – her hair seemed to be crawling. Her long talons were black and thick with dirt, and her face was pasty with weeks of encrusted make-up. And every morning at eleven o'clock she would go up to the end of the boat to be there on time when they opened the hatches, and brought up for air and their daily douche with a sea-water hose, the three thousand Italian prisoners. Although she knew she could not get near any of them she seemed to wallow in the stench of male bodies which had been locked up through the sweltering heat of a tropical night. She would make obscene signs to them and try to excite the poor things. One day one of them tried to get at her and the young guard who had a sten-gun which he was not supposed to have loaded jabbed at the prisoner with the butt of it and a spate of bullets went off right into his own face. I was standing next to him as he fell at my feet, a beautiful young boy now completely mutilated. He was taken to the hospital, and the prisoner was put in chains for the rest of the voyage. The prostitute scuttled away. It was all over so quickly that I was probably the only one who knew what had caused the sense-less accident. But the day that disturbed me the most during those submarine raids, was about five days out at twelve a.m. We were just preparing to go down to our usual rather nasty meal, when a series of depth charges started to shake our boat. Those of us on the deck rushed to the side to see if we could see anything. These attacks were so sinister because all that was evident was this mass of beautiful torquoise water surrounding us on which dipped the impressive battleships looking completely impregnable and yet underneath the water and lurking just out of sight were silent attackers who could destroy us all. Naturally one imagined they were everywhere.

Just at the moment that we were about to give up and go down to dine suddenly a single depth charge, which seemed terrifyingly near, shook us viciously. We all held on to whatever was nearest to us, and as we looked out across the water gradually a circle of black oil belched up from the bowels of the sea, growing larger as we gazed on it and soon became still. It took a little time for everyone to realise that a submarine had been hit and that the oil was the only evidence that remained.

Then cheers broke out, rejoicing, relief, excitement that we had struck first and hit the target.

But as I looked at that circle of black, growing smaller as we sped away from it, I couldn't help feeling sick at the thought of a hundred and fifty men suffering the most horrible death underneath it.

We were, of course, unable to move without our lifebelts. We were made to carry them everywhere, even to the loo. As we neared the equator sleeping in the cabin became unbearable and I was determined to get out somehow. The ship was blacked out and the decks were out of bounds after dark, because of the danger of lighted cigarettes being seen and also because the top decks were gunsights. But I decided I was going to sleep on deck if I could get out. So one night I took a rug and small pillow and made my way to the door that led to the upper boat deck. Strictly out of bounds and I had to pass the brigadier's cabin to get there. I had my hand on the deck door when I heard the Brig coming so I dashed through out on to the deck – but in my hurry I forgot that there is a ledge on all ship's doors and I cracked my shin against it as I fell out on to the dark deck on the other side. It was terribly painful as I gashed the skin off all down the bone. I lay out there in the dark in agony, not daring to go back. I couldn't stay there as I thought someone would fall over me coming through the door – so I dragged myself up the deck stairs on to the boat deck and crawled under one of the big guns. I thought at least it wouldn't go off *at* me if I was *under* it! I was unable to wash the wound and unfortunately some of the soot from the funnel must have got into it as I slept and by the morning it had turned septic. I got downstairs and cleaned it as best I could and stuck the pain as long as I could until I started to run a temperature, then I knew I should go to the ship's doctor. I was embarrassed to go with my comparatively small wound when I thought of the young guard – and all the other desperately ill people in the hospital. However my fever was rising so I went. He started to clean the wound and I lay there trying not to make a fuss. He looked at me and with a sarcastic voice said, "Hah! face registering pain!" I was so furious I kicked the basin out of his hand and leapt off the bed and ran to my cabin. He did have the grace to come after me and apologise and when he saw how awful our cabin was he insisted I be given a bed in the hospital. This was marvellous because I could breathe down there.

That night I woke at three in the morning and said to the matron that I had been dreaming of rats and that I was sure the ship was going down. "Don't worry," she said, "I have been torpedoed three times and I'm still here to tell the tale." And then she pointed to Jim the orderly, a young man with snow-white hair. Jim, she said, had been on a boat that had been hit and had started out in a lifeboat with twenty-six people, and one by one each of them had either died of exposure, gone mad, committed suicide or murdered each other until there were only three left when the boat was picked up outside Freetown. Two had died in hospital and Jim was the sole survivor. When he regained consciousness his hair had turned absolutely white, and yet as soon as he was strong enough he volunteered to go

World Tour programme of
People in love – Noel Coward,
Sir John Gielgud, Tyrone
Power, Peter Ustinov, Bob
Hope, Maurice Chevalier

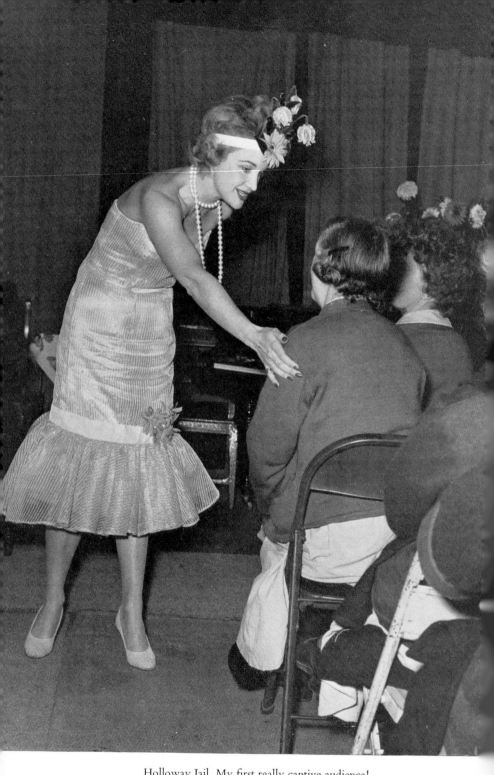

Holloway Jail. My first really captive audience!

back to sea. There were endless stories like this of incredible courage, so that when I used to watch the German planes circling round the convoy just out of reach of the destroyer's guns I found myself thinking how lucky I was to be going to England for purely selfish motives to do something I really wanted to do, and I buried my face thankfully in my volume of Shakespeare.

Of course, there was the enforced gaiety which always runs concurrently with danger. Two very lively and attractive girls, Peter Berry, and Diana Wallinger – whose husband later became British Ambassador in Vienna – led the evening gambols. With the number of men vastly outnumbering the women they certainly had a ball. I had a very sweet and good-looking ship's officer who took me under his wing and I was very happy just to stand at the ship's rails at night and hold his hand, and look into the stygian waters round us. Not that he could have done much in an emergency, but I felt secure with him there. He found me a little unused room down in the hold where I could go and act my heart away with no one near. There was a strange kind of urgency about my wanting to do just that under the circumstances but it seemed to me to be a necessity to have something I believed in to hold on to. Maybe it took the place of praying.

Well, one morning, after three weeks of this strange living, there was great excitement and I rushed out on deck to see what it was, and to my astonishment I saw the Liver birds rising high above the sea haze. We were actually home. Liverpool has never looked more beautiful to me, and I have always had a great affection for it ever since. Suddenly the boat became the most excitable place on earth. The atmosphere was electric. Everyone was running round in disorganised circles. Laughter was indistinguishable from relieved quiet hysteria. No one could believe we had really made it. Life was capable of being lived again after the hiatus at sea. Some were going to be happy, some were not, but at this very moment the simple knowledge that we had been spared to tackle the challenge was the greatest gift we had been given. I couldn't find my little officer to say goodbye to him, my feet were itching to get on to English soil, Peter and Diana were being met by their husbands, hankies were being waved from the quayside, tears of joy were abundant, the three Italian prostitutes who had by now been put under medical supervision walked out proudly at the head of ten stretcher cases, and even the three thousand Italian prisoners seemed happy to be in captivity. Eventually we were all bundled into the boat train and it was only then that we became aware of the devastation that had been wrought in the town and surroundings by the bombing. Momentarily the initial relief and exhilaration of the arrival turned in to a shocked silence. But even that didn't last long because the joy at being alive and in England and in a train rattling towards London was simply indescribable.

I had written to some dear friends to ask if I could stay with them for a few days till I could get a job, so they would be waiting for me in London. I sat back and absorbed the beautiful countryside. It was May and the blossoms were out and although it was 1943, the scars of battle were not too evident out in the country.

When I got to the station in London I couldn't find my friends, but as I was struggling with getting my cases out of the van a very nice looking man of about forty, tall, strong square jaw and very blue eyes, came up to me and said that as my friends had been bombed out of London they had moved to the country and had asked him to take me down to them. He took me first to his flat for a wash and brush up and then we drove down to Suffolk.

Chapter 7

WE arrived at an enchanting fifteenth-century cottage where my friends now lived and as my wound on my leg was still in a cage and not quite healed I was looked after and cosseted and allowed to get over the crossing for all of six weeks during which time I prepared my own offensive to "attack" the West End theatre. I wrote innumerable letters, made a whole series of appointments. Then I sat and waited to be summoned. Absolutely nothing happened at all. All my letters of introduction were politely acknowledged with vague promises of future fulfilment. Appointments were cancelled with monotonous regularity. Now I was beginning to worry. Something had to crack soon. Six weeks was too long to inflict myself on friends, kind as they were. Also Martin, who had met me at the station, was becoming a frequent visitor and was suggesting – very properly – that he could give me his flat in London and he could go and stay with a friend. But these were obligations I was unwilling to accept because I knew even then that this was going to be just the beginning of a tight net in which I was going to get caught. So very firmly I sat down and wrote a story of my experiences on the boat coming over and sent it to the B.B.C. which I hoped would impress them on top of all the other letters I had written to them. Bingo! It worked! Four days later I got a call to say my story had been accepted and would I come up and read it myself at seven p.m. the following Thursday. Thrilled, I took the train and arrived at six-thirty and went to the reception desk. The receptionist told me to go to Studio A at seven p.m. and Studio C at seven-thirty. This mystified me but as I didn't know the ways of the B.B.C. I did as I was told. I read my story from seven to seven-thirty, then rushed unwittingly to Studio C without any idea why, and as I opened the studio door I saw the audience of five hundred and the producer rushed up and said, "You're late, have you got your script?" "No," I said, "are you sure it's me you want?" "Oh Christ! Bloody inefficiency! Can you do it or not?" "Yes, of course," I said, not knowing what it was I was supposed to do. "Right," he said, and shoved the hour-long script in my hand, "You're the compère and you're on the air ten seconds from now!" Well, fortunately I had had radio experience in South Africa so I just gulped hard and plunged in. It was a programme called, "Just What the Doctor Ordered," and it was introducing people from the audience in London to their sick and wounded relatives abroad. Well, I managed to get through it without a mistake and the producer, through sheer relief, was carried away enough to give me a fortnightly contract at five guineas a programme. Independence at last! Now I could afford to pay for a room in London and get down to bearding the agents in their dens.

I was a bit pushed to find a room at my price as I now would have two pounds twelve and six per week on which to live, including everything. However, I managed to get accepted by the Three Arts Club, which was a club for theatrical ladies. There were only about seven rooms, all occupied by, it seemed, character actresses of a certain age. One or two of them didn't suffer me very gladly but were made up for by the sister of Gwen Ffrangcon-Davies, who was a singer and was simply wonderful to me, kind and warm and understanding. I was given a room right on top of the house in Gloucester Place for thirty shillings a week. It did have a hole in the roof through which an unexploded incendiary bomb had gone. But the hole was now covered after a fashion with a piece of hessian and had a permanent bucket underneath. And for another ten shillings a week I got one meal a day. That left me twelve and six for incidentals. I was rich! Now came the business of trailing round agents, producers, etc. I got myself accepted by an agent and soon landed my first job in the theatre at the Playhouse– a play called *Six Pairs of Shoes*, a charming story of the back- and front-stage life of six chorus girls, and we needed a delicate three-piece string orchestra to give the atmosphere of the nightclub and play the numbers we had to do. Somewhere along the line someone got carried away and, instead of the trio, employed Harry Roy and a seventy-five-piece orchestra. Needless to say this unbalanced the show to such an extent that we fell on our faces after three weeks. No discredit to Harry Roy who was splendid but just seventy-two men too many! However, grateful for small mercies I saved my three week's salary to tide me over my next "resting" period. This ran into four months, during which time my figure improved but my shoe leather deteriorated. Although I accepted the lovely meals that Martin bought me, I was trying to ward off the fact that he was in love with me. However, my next job came and I concentrated hard on that. This was a play with Esmé Percy as the star. We rehearsed three weeks with no pay, and we opened and closed in one week. I emerged fifteen pounds richer. But not for long. Walking home in the black-out with my fifteen pounds in my bag I felt a man following me. I thought he was just trying to pick me up so I turned and gave him a filthy look hoping that would deter him, but when I saw the expression on his face I realised it wasn't me he was after. So I started to run but he was quicker and suddenly he grabbed me and then tried to get my handbag. Desperately I clung on to it, knowing it would be a very long time before I'd earn another fifteen pounds, and as he was proving stronger in the tug-of-war I started to scream with all my theatrical vocal power. He soon shut that up with an almighty uppercut and knocked me clean out on the pavement, took my bag and disappeared into the anonymity of the blackout. Fortunately a passing car with three officers in it heard my screams and arrived too late to catch the man but in time to pick me up, bring me round and take me home. So I was back where I started.

Three more months and now a superb part in an amusing play at St. James's Theatre. An innocuous idea which was, briefly, that a mother and two daughters take in two American soldiers and in order that they all may live for the moment and be happy during the bitter war period, they use a scent called Felicity Jasmin and are able to put their past lives into a sort of Limbo until the perfume wears off. Well, somehow the producer managed to make it look or sound more licentious than it was and the Lord Chamberlain decided it was bad for Anglo-American relations, and after the first night banned the play. That opening night was just about one of the most electrifying experiences of my life. It was the time of the doodle-bugs, and up to then I had rather enjoyed watching them come over from my top window in Gloucester Place. I would wait until I could hear the engine cut out and then in the ten seconds that remained before they exploded I would slide down the banisters of the five flights and land in the basement just as the whole house shook from the extended blast.

But this night was very different. We had got to within ten minutes of the final curtain, the play had not been going very well and I had a line to say which was, "Now, now, enough of all this nonsense." Someone from the gallery shouted, "Hear! Hear!" And just as the rest of the gallery were about to join in, the sirens went. There was a moment of stunned silence, then a mumbling restlessness from the audience trying to decide whether to go or stay. I kept thinking, "This is our first night, we can't stop now." Then we all heard the doodle-bug approaching. As the noise got louder I thought this one was getting uncomfortably close. It got closer and the noise was now deafening. I hoped it meant it was going to pass over the theatre but suddenly we all clearly heard the engine cut out – and realised we had ten seconds left before we knew the worst. They were the longest I've ever lived through. Panic set in in the audience, some screamed, others climbed under the seats, others put their coats over their heads. The atmosphere was tense with terror. The lady who was playing my mother exited rather quickly, leaving me alone up there, but all I kept thinking was we must go on, we must go on. So I went on talking, not knowing what I was saying and talking louder and louder to try to stop the strange unearthly vibrations that were coming from the audience. Then it struck. It had landed just behind us in Pall Mall, but being an old theatre all the dust of decades, pieces of scenery and debris hurtled down in a great cloud. I was covered from head to foot, but we were, thank God, all alive, so, ridiculously and incongruously, we continued to act the last five minutes of the play. The curtain came down, and I suppose through sheer relief the audience really let themselves go. When the curtain rose again for us to take the usual curtain call, the atmosphere was unbelievable, half the theatre cheering and half booing. High-pitched hysterical laughter mixed with jerky sobbing. There was nothing we, the actors, could do except stand there and take it on the chin. Gradually the theatre emptied and we were alone. But we knew as we dragged ourselves back to our dressing rooms that in spite of the circumstances the audience had not had a highly satisfactory evening! And so another set of neons were put out.

That made three flops in a row for me and my confidence was beginning to wear a bit thin.

Chapter 8

Now it was assessment time. I had been in England about eighteen months. And I had just had my twentieth birthday. It was a rather sad one because I had to face up to the fact that I had not so far been an unqualified success. All I still had was – happily – my radio programme which kept the rent paid, but everything else had fallen round me. I had refused to accept anything from Martin because I didn't want to aggravate an already impossible situation. He was divorced. He was one of the most wonderful men I have ever met. He loved me with a deep, unselfish, yet at the same time highly possessive love, and wanted to marry me. And I began to get frightened of what he might do if ever I left him. During my birthday dinner he told me that if he could have three years of my life he would be able to die happily. It was then that I made the mental decision that as I had youth on my side, and I was rich in time, I could afford to sacrifice that period in return for the kind of love that many women dream about. The fact that I was not in love with him was as hurtful to me as it was painful to him. To try and make up for it, although I was not living with him, I devoted all my free time to trying to give him the kind of happiness he had never known. I made no other friends as he was extremely jealous and kept me very closely guarded. But I didn't mind as my theatre interests consumed all my thoughts.

It was about this time that my agent told me they were auditioning for the new season at Stratford-on-Avon, and that he had made an appointment for me. Now my knowledge of Shakespeare was practically nil apart from three or four famous speeches that I had learnt specifically for audition purposes. But I had hardly read any of the plays right through purely and simply because I didn't understand them. So I went to the audition in more than a little trepidation. There seemed to be masses of young girls and boys milling about waiting to be called. Then my turn came, and I thought this time it's "do or die", so I threw myself into the potion scene from *Romeo and Juliet* and acted my little heart out. I pulled out all the stoppers and let rip. Well it seemed to work the oracle because darling old Robert Atkins came down to the footlights and said, "That was very good, have you played much Shakespeare?" "Oh yes," I lied, "masses," adding hastily, "In Africa, of course." "Right," he said. "Refresh yourself on Olivia's speech from *Twelfth Night* and come back tomorrow." Elated I went home and tried to learn Olivia's speech. I couldn't make head or tail of it. I sat up all night just getting the words into my head and when I got to the audition the next morning, very unsure of myself, I found to my horror he had all the management side concerned with the season sitting in a row waiting to hear me, but by a stroke of incredible luck he only asked me to do the potion scene again, and not the other. So again I flung myself into it. When I had finished he turned to the others and said, "I think we'll give her the job." Then he said, "I hope you realise what this involves – we do eight plays and you will be playing six leading roles which are Juliet, Desdemona, Olivia, Anne Bullen, Charmian and Kate Hardcastle, the other two roles of Cleopatra and Beatrice will be played by American actress Claire Luce. We start rehearsals in three months and I want you word perfect by then. I am taking a tremendous chance on you and I don't wish to be let down. So go home and start studying today."

I went home in a trance. Got up to my room and it suddenly hit me what I had undertaken. I had never read any of these plays. I didn't even know which play most of the parts came out of. It was all very well bluffing him on one role of Juliet, but how was I going to cope? I went to the phone to tell him I had bitten off more than I could chew, that I had never played Shakespeare, etc., etc., but a little voice inside me kept saying – "Come on, you can do it." Three times I went to the phone, three times I stopped at the crucial moment – and finally I determined to take the bit between my teeth and have a go. So I got down to work. I found out who was the best Shakespearian scholar in London to help me to learn and know what I was going to be talking about, and the best voice man, so that when I understood the words I could then project them in that large theatre. I hadn't the money for this so I borrowed it from Martin promising to pay back so much out of my salary each week. Fortunately I found Dr. Hock who was a very old but fabulous teacher and had been with Reinhardt, and he opened up a whole new world for me by teaching me how to understand Shakespeare in the simplest terms. So for three months I closeted myself and studied and worked on my voice with Bertie Scott and generally prepared myself for this incredible break. The great day eventually dawned when we opened at Stratford on Avon. Of course it was not the civilised way of working then that it is now. We did a different play for every performance, which meant rehearsing, say *Antony and Cleopatra* in the morning, playing a matinée of *Othello* and an evening show of *Romeo and Juliet*. But I just breathed in every moment of it. It was food and drink to me. I was in my element as I had never been before. It was the first time in my life that I really felt fulfilled. And thanks to my wonderful tutors my notices as each play was premiered were fortunately very good. So this meant I had put my foot on the first rung of the precarious theatrical ladder. Stratford was an inspiring place in which to work and as it was the last year of the war – 1945 – there were a lot of servicemen who used to come to see the plays. The British Council gave lectures for the public before going to see the plays. I used to attend these. At question time afterwards there were always amusing incidents. One young American stood up after the lecture on Henry VIII and very eagerly asked, "Say can you tell me, Ma'am, does Henry VIII go through all his wives this afternoon?" Another one asked me where I hid the onion that I rubbed on my eyes to make me cry in the death scene.

One night when I was playing the balcony scene the stage-hands had forgotten to secure the balcony to the supporting flat. And as I leant on it to sigh "Ah! Me!" the entire balcony came away and I was left balancing very undignifiedly on my tummy on the balustrade. I and the balcony swayed right over the footlights and I was caught by the stage-hands just before being shot into the fourth row of the stalls.

So for a whole year I worked and enjoyed every second of it. I was earning twenty-five pounds a week and soon had made enough money to buy a little car. I bought it at an auction sale in Birmingham for a hundred and twenty-five pounds, a Morris Minor and it was a gem. I sold it three years later for three hundred and fifty pounds! But while I had it, it gave me enormous freedom and pleasure. I used to tear up to London most weekends. Petrol rationing was still on so I made friends with an American officer who had a jeep and promised me some petrol out of it. He told me to meet him in a little lane behind the theatre and said that if I brought a tube of rubber he would transfer the petrol from one car to the other. I searched the whole of Stratford for a tube of rubber without success – and determined not to miss this golden opportunity I duly arrived in the chosen spot with the nearest thing to a rubber tube I could find. Actually it was an enema. The embarrassment the poor man suffered as I watched him squeezing this wretched enema in and out!

It was about this time that I met my husband-to-be for the first time. An author who was writing a book on celebrities asked me to lunch with him at the Ritz so he could do a chapter on me. I accepted and on my arrival at the Ritz was introduced to his other guest the Vicomte d'Orthez. He was supremely good-looking and full of charm and sophistication. He bent down and kissed my hand. That for a start filled me with suspicion. I froze. I had been brought up in a very sheltered background and to me all Frenchmen had only one idea in their heads, which was to charm you, then drug you, then carry you off and sell you to the white slave traffic. And that I was determined was not going to happen to me. So I studiously and politely avoided any attention he paid me, rather proudly impressing him that I wasn't such easy meat as perhaps I looked! Immediately after lunch I made some pretext of getting away to another appointment. I left and never gave him another thought, little realising that I was to meet him again a year later. But before that year was up I was sent a copy of the book in which my host wrote a chapter on that luncheon. Here are some rather extravagant extracts from what he had written. (The picture printed with them appears opposite p. 14.)

"Inured to the possession of physical perfection and a mind soignée . . . the first of these inherited, the second appropriated . . . accepting these precious possessions graciously, living with them naturally, Moira Lister is an upburst of intense life held to a graceful trot . . . stimulated by, and practising the Art of the serious Theatre: unhampered by apprehension, Miss Lister is prospecting progressively the muggy alleyways of backstage with the easy dominance of one supremely conscious of ultimate sovereign success.

"Moira's slender five feet and five inches glow with the pour of the tropic sun; the hair is pollen, cascading gently with the glow of the chestnut bloom in June . . . to the eye as the perfume of May blossom to the nostrils . . . the brow is serene, the fragile nose a toy jetty separating two opaque eddies in a sunlit archipelago . . . the mouth is firm, contributing to the sum of conversation and not laming it with illicit questions and immoral giggles . . . Moira's interest is contained, her smile is rare and as glad as the song of the Nightingale . . . her cigarette is

76

ornamental and her quota of alcohol untouched and, as she reads this you can hear her say . . . 'Oh dear, doesn't sound a bit like me'. . . Maybe not, dear lady, it's like hearing your voice speak to you for the first time via the sound-track.

RITZ RESTAURANT

"Miss Lister arrived charmingly late, a chapeau lodged on her *châtain* locks just like the circumflex on that letter *â*, and, suspensory, a waft of tulle that refracted the lustre emanating from her features.

" 'Moira, may I present the Vicomte Jacques d'Orthez?' "

" 'Jacques, I should like . . .'

"When the actress had brushed aside her tulle impediment and manifested forth her glory, her two servitors had been filled with admiration and had gazed at her openly, marvelling at such perfection and grace; and that in the Ritz Restaurant, where beauty, casual deportment and fine raiment are un-rationed. Lacking orchestra, ethereous . . . with the shafted light flooding through the casements and diamond-drops pinned in the roof-gloom, the salon presented a spectacle compared with which the most brilliant scene in a big Musical would have appeared artificial . . . The heroine, rising twenty-two, *rayonnante, ravissante, douée d'une sensibilité excessive*, stabilising the dangerously slack-wire of verbal badinage with astonishing aplomb.

"The hero, *trente-six, suave, dilettante, débonnaire*, inexorably filtering the conversation into, and out of, tropical temperatures *avec une finesse incomparable*."

And so on, and so on!

Reading it now so many years later, it seems very high-falutin, but it is certainly a unique record of a first meeting!

So I finished my year at Stratford and came back to London with enough money saved to find and furnish a little flat and

77

live a more normal sort of life. I found a flat in Baker's Mews. It cost me three pounds five a week. It was tiny but ideal – with a garage in which I could put my little treasure, and above I had a little drawing room, a dining room, a bedroom, kitchen and bath. Now at last I would be able to get my beloved mother to stay with me for as long as she wanted. I was so sad she had missed my Stratford season because it was the realisation of all her dreams and, through her, mine. However, just as I had it all ready, I got another super job. To play the juvenile lead in John Clements and Kay Hammond's first actor-manager venture, playing two gorgeous parts – Palmyra in *Marriage à la mode* by Dryden and *The Kingmaker*. We were to tour for thirteen weeks, then play at the St. James's Theatre (I couldn't wait to eradicate the memory of the last time I played there) and then tour again for sixteen weeks. This I adored because it gave me the chance to see the country, as we were still unable to get abroad immediately after the war, and it meant a year's work. It was a wonderful year. Katie was adorable and John a superb boss in every way. I learnt so much about comedy by watching Katie. She was such a wonderful comedienne; no one has ever taken her place.

Sundays were train calls when we travelled from one town to another. And it was also poker school time. John and Katie were inveterate gamblers and great poker players. I knew nothing of the game and stood behind Katie trying to learn. She was sitting there with an implacable expression and very lucky hands and couldn't understand why John kept winning until she realised that he wasn't looking at *her* poker face *but at mine*, which was unconsciously reflecting every card Katie held. I was forthwith banished from the poker school.

Everywhere we went I used to go straight to the antique shops trying to find bargains for my little flat. Many of the things I bought then I still have today, and their value has gone up a hundred-fold. David Peel who was my Romeo and also juvenile lead with me in these plays started his collection of priceless antiques and has since been running a highly successful antique business in Bond Street.

When I came back to London I was offered the title role of *The Trial of Mary Dugan* which was being done for a limited season at Richmond. I took it because after two years of the classics I thought it was time for a modern play. The play was very successful and I remember the production more because it noted the second abortive meeting with my husband-to-be, now one year later. After the performance one night my dresser told me there were two gentlemen to see me. She showed them in. The Vicomte himself and his best friend, one of the Dormeuil boys – another Frenchman! They said they had enjoyed the play and would be very honoured if they could drive me back to London and take me out to dinner. Again I froze – drive back to London alone in a car with *two* Frenchmen! I would obviously be raped twice and *then* shipped off to the white slave traffic!! I politely declined the offer on the pretext that I already had a date. In fact I took the tube home by myself and cooked my own supper. Another year passed before I was to meet him again. The Fates were certainly playing funny games with me!

My three years I had mentally put aside for Martin were now up but I didn't have the courage to break away because I was afraid of the reaction. So I let things drift on. Now that I was back in London my mother came over from South Africa, and she very soon saw that my life was not all that it appeared to be. She was disturbed to find my permanent escort was twenty-five years older than I, and that I had no friends to speak of. She arranged that I should go to Switzerland alone for two weeks and, as she put it, have some fun. So rather reluctantly I went off to Crans-Sur-Sierre. That trip changed the course of my life. I met a young medical student of my age, who is now incidently a professor and a very famous surgeon in Italy – he couldn't speak English and I couldn't speak French, but as we skied all day and danced all night words were superfluous. I suddenly realised that I had been behaving and thinking and feeling like a woman twice my age. Here in the Swiss mountains I laughed, did nonsense things, behaved as a girl of twenty-one should and was like a bird let out of a cage. And because of this awakening in me, I knew I must make the break with Martin otherwise I was doomed. So I wrote him a long letter trying to explain how I felt and trying to hurt him as little as I could. I knew it would be a cruel moment for him but I had to do it. I posted the letter begging him never to see me again and not to contact me because it would be easier to make an absolutely clean break. When I arrived back in London there he was at the airport, gay, loving, happy to see me, ready to drive me home. I got into the car while I was trying to work out his reaction but it was when we were halfway home I realised he had not yet received my letter. My heart sank. He sensed there was something wrong and questioned me. My courage deserted me again and I simply said, "I have written you a letter. You must wait until you read it." But I could feel the cold sweat on my forehead. He dropped me and when he got back to his flat the letter had arrived. If I hadn't had my mother there to give me strength I could never have gone through with it. It was a horrible time, but gradually he got over it and realised that it was all over. It seemed so unfair that he should have to suffer just because he loved me and had only helped me and been wonderful to me. I had a tremendous affection for him, and still have. But had we married it would have been disaster. So the moment had come for a new phase in my life.

And to begin it I went into a kind of voluntary retreat. For six months I saw no one, went nowhere. I used to rise at six, go to Mass, then walk through Regent's Park and back, write, play my little piano, in I suppose a subconscious effort to prove to myself that I had not left Martin for anyone else, but because it was the right thing to do. I was also afraid of new relationships because I didn't seem to know how to handle them and they only seemed to bring me unhappiness. I even let beautiful Howard Keel slip through my fingers! He was very keen on me and I was so cold and withdrawn on every occasion he took me out that in the end he gave up. That didn't help either! And it was at the end of this kind of purifying process of my life that I nearly lost it altogether.

Chapter 9

I RELUCTANTLY accepted an invitation to go to a nightclub in London with some theatre friends and while I was dancing I heard someone say, "Moira, how marvellous to see you." I looked up and there was a very handsome blond, blue-eyed friend of mine from South Africa, called, as he was then, George Armstrong. I was very thrilled to see him. He lived next door to us in Johannesburg and was an Englishman who had married my school-friend Liz. He was a Squadron Leader and we had been to many parties together in South Africa and although I didn't know him terribly well, he was always fun and gay and full of amusing stories. He asked me to join him for a drink and we started talking. I asked how Liz was and his face fell. He told me that she had been killed in a car smash on the Pretoria Road, and that he was over here in England looking for agencies to take back to South Africa so that he could give his son a good education. I can remember distinctly my reaction was, "Well, you are so attractive and now a widower with a beautiful little boy – I wouldn't mind marrying you!" Fortunately in the light of what followed I didn't express my thoughts. However, he put my name and address in his little book – later to become very famous – and said he would ring me and take me out to dinner. I was delighted. I went home and wrote to my sister in South Africa saying I had seen George Armstrong and how awful that Liz had been killed, etc. Two months later he rang me and asked me to dine. We went to the Bagatelle, spent a wonderful evening laughing and dancing. He behaved impeccably, drove me home, kissed me on both cheeks and said goodbye and left.

The next day I received a letter from my sister saying "For God's sake are you out of your mind? George Armstrong is Neville Heath!" Bombshell! I simply didn't believe it. I was convinced she had made a mistake. Because in fact the papers here had not published a picture of him after the first murder, I had no yardstick by which to judge except my own instinct about the man. He was charming, gay, absolutely nothing salacious about him. And I could have as easily become one of his victims as either of the girls he so brutally murdered. Obviously because of the family ties with his wife in Johannesburg the police must have contacted her for enquiries and therefore the awareness of his identity was common knowledge in South Africa whereas in England he was still just a name. However, I continued to believe in him completely until, after the second murder in the Bournemouth Chines, his picture was published in the paper. I can still see it now. Curly blond hair neatly combed, a slight smile and those ice-blue eyes – I knew they were blue because I had looked at them very deeply – a smart suit, and there he was handcuffed and on his way to be hanged. I felt quite sick. I still found it impossible to equate the savage abnormal sexual murders he had done with the charming man who had taken me out on the town. This must have been the quintessence of the behaviour of the schizophrenic. I felt sure if he had walked into my room at that moment and explained to me that there had been a horrible mistake, and that he was innocent, I would have believed him.

But in fact he had already committed one murder. Ten days later he committed his second murder – so I had been sandwiched in for dinner between two murders. The only thing that may have saved me is that I am blonde and both girls were brunettes. But since writing this, which is from memory of twenty years ago, I have checked with the press files on this case and in fact it makes even more frightening reading when I realise how close I was to being a victim of a sadistic sex murderer.

Here is a brief breakdown of his background:

He was born in 1917 and educated in Essex. He left school at seventeen and a half and got a short service commission in the R.A.F. in 1936. One year later he was court-martialled for the first time for being absent without leave and other offences. He was dismissed from the R.A.F. Three months later he was put on probation for two years for obtaining credit by fraud and eight other offences were taken into consideration. During that two years' probation he committed ten other offences, including theft of jewellery and obtaining clothes by forged bankers' order. He was sentenced to three years' Borstal treatment. He only served a year when war broke out and he was released to join the R.A.S.C. Six months later he was commissioned and posted to the Middle East. But he was unable or unwilling to curb his criminal instincts and within another year he was court-martialled and cashiered for fraudently obtaining a second pay-book and five other charges respecting dishonoured cheques. He embarked for the United Kingdom and, incredibly, "jumped ship" in Durban, went to Johannesburg where he masqueraded as Captain Selway, M.C. (no less!), and passed dishonoured cheques. When things started to hot up he changed his name to George Armstrong, enlisted in the South African Air Force and got a commission! Three months later, in December 1942, he married my girl-friend next door and it was at this period that I met him with my sister and we were both taken by his extreme good looks, wit and charm! Several parties were held at Inanda Polo Club where everyone, or all the girls at least, were vying for his favours. Two years later he was seconded to the R.A.F. In October 1945 he was divorced for desertion, happily for Liz. In December he was court-martialled again – six charges for wearing military decorations without authority – and dismissed from the service. In 1946 in February he returned to the United Kingdom. In April of that year I met him at the Milroy where he told me the lies about Liz being killed in a motor smash. (She is still alive today and has happily remarried.) He wrote my name in his book with a promise to take me out to dinner. Knowing nothing of all this fantastic background, I was delighted. Only two months later, on June 20th, he murdered Mrs. Margery Gardener at Pembridge Court Hotel, Notting Hill. He suffocated her, whipped her viciously and indecently assaulted her. The poker he used is I believe in Scotland Yard's chamber of horrors. No picture was published of him in the papers. On June 23 he travelled to Bournemouth and stayed in the name of Group Captain Rupert Brooke! During the period between June 23 and July 3rd (when he murdered Miss Doreen Marshall) he came up to London and took me out! We spent the evening I have already described at the Bagatelle, after which he went back to Bournemouth and, on July 3rd, met and later that night murdered Doreen Marshall, a W.R.N., in a lonely part of Branksome Chine. He cut her throat, mutilated her and savagely wounded her body; stole her property, pawned her ring and watch. On July 8th he was arrested and taken to London where he was formally charged with both murders. He was convicted, and on October 24th he was executed.

The whole defence of the case rested on a plea of insanity, there being no dispute as to the facts of the murders for which Heath was tried. On the information divulged in the evidence it was established quite clearly that Heath was intelligent, extremely attractive to women, efficient, personable, of good appearance, physique, and of considerable charm. But he was also a cad, liar, a cheat, a brazen mountebank, a cold-blooded egoist and a savage pervert. In psychiatric terms he was a psychopath.

Heath showed a complete lack of remorse, which fact the defence tried to use as evidence of mental abnormality.

Heath's last words before execution, according to a certain paper, were alleged to be, having asked the prison governor for a whisky, "You might make it a double."

So once again my guardian angel, or whoever it is who guides my destiny, plucked me from disaster.

But to show how fine the dividing line between sanity and insanity is, or more precisely the power of the subconscious over the conscious, about this time something happened to me which could have landed me in the most appalling trouble. Bewildered as I am about it, I tell it exactly as it happened.

After the heartbreaking time I had gone through with Martin and having just come out the other side, I met a man who, if only the timing had been different, could probably have been the only man in my life. But I was smarting under the responsibility of Martin's illness due to my rejection of him, and this beautiful creature, who was a cross between Tyrone Power and a dimple Haig, and if he ever reads this will know exactly what I mean, was just surfacing after a disastrous first marriage. Neither of us was able to cope with a new situation. So we had a few months of firm friendship after which he disappeared to America and out of my life. But we danced very often and it was during one of these evenings that I behaved in this extraordinary way. It was New Year's Eve and we had already been to several parties and ended up for the last gasp of the Old Year at the same nightclub where I had encountered Neville Heath called The Milroy. We had had a fair amount to drink, and as I was not a great consumer of alcohol, t had begun to tell more than somewhat. But I do not know whether it was my upbringing or the reaction of the liquor, but the more I drank the straighter my back became and the more dignified I appeared, only by this time amnesia had set in and although I was behaving like anyone's "maiden aunt" I remembered absolutely nothing of my behaviour. Apparently I swept into the Ladies' Room, and happily for me, Madame Pee Pee knew me and really saved me later, for I went to the rail of fur coats (I was still wearing my tweed, as fur was way out of my reach) and to Madame Pee Pee's astonishment I picked out the best mink and put it on my back. I was by now acting entirely at the command of my subconscious, my conscious mind had got lost in the last glass of champagne. I had obviously always wanted a mink and now that I had nothing to restrain me I saw absolutely no harm in obeying the dictates of my subconscious, which was obviously dying for me to own a mink. But worse was to come. As I got to the door of the Ladies' Room, sporting my new acquisition, the owner of the mink arrived! Now dear Madame Pee Pee rushed up and said, "Don't take any notice of Miss Lister, she's only having a game. Come along, dear, put on your tweed, it's much warmer than that old mink." Apparently I complied and went home completely and utterly oblivious of the fact that I could have been clapped in jail for cleptomania at the drop of a mink coat. I knew nothing of what I had done until it was recounted to me the next day. I was horrified. In despair I rang the woman and apologised profusely. She was terribly kind and said I'd given a very good performance. But it frightened the life out of me to discover how easily one can lose all sense of responsibility and lucidity under the influence of alcohol.

Chapter 10

NINETEEN-FORTY-SEVEN and my first big break into the West End. I had just returned from a year's tour with John Clements and Kay Hammond, and heard that auditions were being held for a leading lady for Noel Coward's *Present Laughter*. It was a glamorous role, so I ran round to a milliner I knew and borrowed an enormous black hat, combed my long blonde hair down on my shoulders, put on a simple black dress and prepared to go to the audition which was at three p.m. I was ready by twelve-thirty when the phone went and darling Frances Rowe, who was in the last season with me, suggested we lunch at the Ivy. I thought it was a great idea to take my mind off the terror of the audition, so agreed, explaining I had an appointment (very secretive I was) at three p.m. She said that suited her well as she too had a three p.m. appointment. I arrived at the Ivy rather over-dressed for lunch, stunned to find Fanny in a superb mink coat. Neither of us were very affluent at the time. I didn't mention her coat and she didn't mention my hat, but neither had gone unnoticed. (Her mink, I discovered later, had been borrowed from Katie Hammond.) We finished lunch and both took individual taxis, and more than surprised both turned up at the Haymarket simultaneously, very embarrassingly both going for the same job!

Great credit to Fanny that she has remained a dear friend ever since.

I went on to the stage and there was the Master himself sitting in the stalls. He asked why I looked so brown. I told him I'd just returned from ski-ing. "Well, I hope you didn't get them up your nose," was his comment. That broke the ice (not to mix a metaphor!) and everything went marvellously. He asked me to his house next day to read again for the backers and management, etc. And then he told me the job was mine. I could scarcely contain myself till I got out into the street and when I did I let out the loudest and longest "Yippee" that Ebury Street has ever heard. Working with Coward was really my first taste of champagne. When he was on stage the atmosphere was like a shower of bursting bubbles. Nothing ever threw him or took him by surprise. His wit was razor-sharp. But my being a product of darkest Africa I was completely and utterly overawed by him. I was terrified almost to talk to him as everything I said seemed so banal and trite that I kept my mouth firmly shut, and worshipped at a distance. So that when he sent for me on the first night in London ten minutes before curtain up I immediately feared the worst. However, when I entered his dressing room with every bone in my body quietly rattling, he said, "Moira, I'm very pleased with you, you've done an excellent job so far and I'd like to make you a little present." I was overcome. "No, no, no," I mumbled. "Such an honour to work with you," etc., etc. "No, I insist," he said. He went to his dressing table and took a tiny bottle of perfume called Caron Can-Can from it. The bottle was half empty. He handed it to me with a magnaminous gesture. "There you are my dear, that is for you. *I* have used the other half." I accepted with deep gratitude, feeling that I had never been more flattered in all my life. We ran for two years at the Haymarket and so many amusing things happened during that time they are almost a book in themselves. One night Joyce Carey missed her entrance and Noel and I were alone on stage. The stage manager, not knowing that Miss Carey was still up in her dressing room, rang the front-door bell on cue for her entrance. On cue Noel went to open the door, discovered no Joyce Carey, so closed the door again turned to me without a moment's hesitation and said, "Silly little boys, ringing bells and running away!" Then he

89

took me by the hand, sat me on the settee and said, "Now you come from South Africa. Teach me Zulu!" So for the next few minutes while Joyce Carey was brought down I taught him the rudiments of Zulu!

During our famous love scene, just before the big kiss, frequently he would warn me beforehand that he had eaten garlic. So as his lips almost met mine he would say under his breath, "Now – breathe out!"

If we had a particularly stodgy matinée as I made my entrance he would say, "Don't expect a laugh from this lot, they're all suffering from the change!"

But probably the greatest memory I have of him is his unselfishness as an actor. He always fed other people's laughs superbly. He never tried to outdo anyone else on the stage. He wanted everyone to give full value to his lines as an author, and to complement his performance as an actor. I learnt a great deal of the technique of timing from him.

There was a great social aura that surrounded him. The Duchess of Kent was a frequent visitor. So was her sister. At the parties he used to give at his home, all the crowned heads of the theatre and Hollywood would flock. There I met so many wonderful and talented people. Bob Hope, whom I was later to work with. Loretta Young, gorgeous-looking. Douglas Fairbanks, whose leading lady I was to become. It was a fabulous two years for me although I was still very much a greenhorn so didn't benefit from it nearly as much as I should have. I was still hiding behind an insecurity that only left me as I walked on to a stage.

And it was about this time that the big moment, and necessary one in my private life, was about to take shape. I was to meet again for the third time in three years, my future husband. I was walking down Jermyn Street and suddenly bumped into him. He was his usual gay, charming self, delighted to see me, kissed my hand, and happily for me – having now been to France and Switzerland, I had discovered that all Frenchmen were not actively concerned with the white slave traffic – I was able to accept this gesture for what it was worth. I was also proud to be able to use the few more words of French I had learnt. I was beginning to become slightly more civilised. We chatted for a few minutes and went on our various ways. About two months later I had a letter from him, asking if he might give my name to a French fashion house that was starting up in London as they would like to invite celebrities to their opening. At the end of the letter was a P.S. "We really must have that lunch one day." I wrote back a short note saying he could give my name to his friends.

Now about this time I had made a Peter Cheyney film called *Uneasy Terms* with Michael Rennie. This was made while I was still playing at the Haymarket in *Present Laughter*, and the night of the première arrived. A big party was being given at the Savoy for Michael and me. As I was still playing in the theatre I was only able to join them after the film. My elder sister was over from South Africa at the time and I was trying to think of someone to take her to the party. Perhaps that French Vicomte would be a good idea! He accepted readily, and it was only when I was on stage that night that I found myself wondering what he was like. Because I had never really taken much notice of him. He was a name without a face. Was he short or tall? Handsome or not? Would he be fun or a bore? However, the questions were soon to be answered. After the performance my dresser announced there was a Vicomte d'Orthez to see me. She opened the door and in walked one of the best-looking men I'd ever met. Tall, dark and handsome was no cliché for him. I was stunned. I stood and stared while electric current whisked its way through my veins, stopped at my knees and I sat down limply! It was precisely at that moment that I fell in love with him. I dressed in a flurry of excitement, and off we drove to the Savoy. To get there we had to pass Leicester Square where my picture was showing. In front of the theatre was an enormous hoarding with a larger than life-size picture of me lying draped on a couch doing the seductive bit, and underneath written the words "Beautiful but Beware". I laughed as I thought how the wheel had come full circle. We spent a wonderful first evening. My sister very kindly did the honours with Michael Rennie, happily, because I saw no one but my Gascon Cavalier!

From that moment he never left my side and never has. I owe him so much. He taught me so many things. Mainly laughter. I had cried a lot before I met him and my tears were not over but he showed me how to curb my hypersensitivity, and how unbecoming pettiness was. And I suppose the most important thing was his belief in me. This gave me the security I needed. The knowledge that no matter how bad my day had been, and in this profession there are very bad days, I knew I could go home and he would be there to comfort me and then to laugh and show me how unimportant it was because he believed I had so much going for me, that tomorrow a whole new world would be there, with me on its threshold. He encouraged every aspect of my meagre talents, so that my days became filled with new achievements. No horizon was too far to reach. He stirred my inventiveness, my creativeness, until I began to feel that I could tackle almost anything. This of course had its dangers because very often I got carried away and tried to do things of which I was really not capable: such as starting a dress business as a sideline, which was a disaster, swallowing a large slice of my savings. Then some years later buying an enormous house which we were incapable of running and getting badly into debt. But in spite of these setbacks life was full and fun and exciting. That was the credit side but as always there is the reverse of the coin. He had been seventeen years in the glamorous French Cavalry, a Spahi tearing up the dust of the African Desert on the back of a camel. Life up till the war was a gay ball of totting up the medals (he has eleven) under his Burnous, (the great cape of the French Cavalry's uniform). Then his father died and he discovered his inheritance had been whittled away on slow horses and fast women.

The war came and he was taken prisoner. Undaunted he designed glamorous life-size ladies along the walls next to the beds of the German officers, while discovering the best escape routes which he very soon used. He got back to Paris, was betrayed by a French woman who saw he was still wearing prisoner-of-war boots and he was taken away again and locked up, but three months later, having got on whatever side was necessary of the milk-maid, was hidden by her in the milk-cart, and away to freedom once more. He got to Lisbon and from there to London. So that by the time he met me he had only a very modest job and understandably was unwilling to take on the responsibility of marriage and children without the proper financial accoutrements. I on my side was secretly afraid of launching into a sophisticated world about which I knew nothing, and for which I didn't particularly care, as I still had a long period of adaptation to suffer. I am, off the stage, an introvert by nature, so bottling up emotions is the easy way out. Jacques, happily, is the opposite, so the balance is ideal. So although marriage was an accepted eventuality, the present was a very necessary "getting to know you" period.

Fortunately he wanted me to continue my career because he had the foresight to avoid being caged up with a frustrated, unfulfilled actress. So when the offer to go to America and star opposite Jack Buchanan in *Don't Listen, Ladies* came, we both thought it was a good thing to do however much we missed each other.

Hardy Amies made me the most beautiful wardrobe for the play and we rehearsed in London before leaving. Jack Buchanan was an enchanting man. Kind, shy, warm and a real pro. He always rehearsed with his hat on, claiming he felt more secure under it! He was so unselfish that as he opened the play with a very long soliliquy, he never wanted to have people waiting around while he rehearsed it alone, with the result that when we opened at a pre-New York week in Brighton, the poor soul was extremely under-rehearsed. Consequently he dried after the third line, but enchantingly went up to the prompt corner and said, "I say, old boy, could I have the lines loud and clear." The prompter obliged but as is the custom was neither loud or, through fear, clear! So Jack simply stood on the front of the stage, and said, "Louder and clearer, old boy!" That, of course, endeared him to the audience and he was away.

We went over to New York – my first visit – in luxury on the *Queen Elizabeth*. This was a great experience for me. I was very happy dining in the great restaurant, but Jack insisted on inviting me to the Starlight Room (or some such name) which was extremely expensive and where all meals were specially ordered. To my dismay the only thing he ordered was steak and kidney pudding, which he adored, and which I must admit they made superbly. We rehearsed on the boat and when we arrived a barrage of cameramen was there to meet us, and insisted I climb on a lot of trunks and give them the "cheese-cake", "show the legs, gal, more! more!" When I had reached what I considered the limit and refused to go higher they lost interest in me and leapt at the next lady and gave her the same treatment, only she happened to be an American Senator!

I arrived at the Savoy Plaza to find an enormous suite had been booked for me, for which naturally I had to pay. This was filled with flowers, with cases of Three Roses Whiskey, with cosmetics, with all the advertising of a commercial world, even down to a packet of babies' diapers (which I found very useful for removing my make-up). I had a large double bedroom (utterly wasted!) a huge lounge and a kitchen. After the press conferences were over, my Scottish blood rose at the thought of all those precious dollars being frittered away just on accommodation and I approached the management to change my suite for just a nice bedroom. This they did, until the play opened and the notice to quit was put up after the first act, because the play was written by Sacha Guitry – a so-called

Nazi collaborationist and Walter Winchell printed the head-lines, "I hope he chokes on his first royalties." Back I went to the management and asked for a single room. This I got until I fell into the hands of a confidence trickster and had to change my single room into a smaller single room, which I think was a converted linen closet! I was sitting in my better single room one day when the phone went and a very cultured voice said how sorry he was to see my play had not been a success and he would like to help me. I sensed danger and refused. A very hurt voice pleaded that I didn't understand, it was simply that he knew what it was like to be a stranger in a foreign land with no one to turn to in distress. He was not asking for a date, was simply going to try and help me leave America with a bundle of notes with which I could buy myself a fur coat (my ears pricked up immediately), and that he didn't even want to meet me or even that I should give him the money (my ears were now above my head). "Go on," I said trying to remain calm. He explained he was a horse owner and trainer and had two fillies running in California that afternoon. He advised me to gather every penny I had left, and give them to the little red-headed pageboy called Anthony, who took all the bets for the hotel, and by six o'clock I would be in clover. But not to do anything for one hour because he wanted to get the very latest information from the course before the race. I paced the room for an hour, terribly tempted, slightly wary, but he sounded so plausible and considerate about me, and sure enough, one hour later he rang, told me not to touch the first horse as it had gone lame, but to put everything on the second, said good luck and rang off. Well, having had my first easy win in South Africa, I thought it was always like that – I took the lift down-stairs and found the little page with the red hair and hotel uniform and gave him very nearly all the dollars I had left. He accepted them and told me he would meet me in the lobby at six p.m. I went off happily to see a matinee of *The Madwoman of Chaillot* (very apt!). After the performance I went to see

Martita Hunt and the first thing she asked me was whether I'd had a call from an Englishman about horses, because she had just been caught for five hundred dollars. My stomach landed with a thump on the floor. Yes, I said, but how does he work, what's the racket? Apparently the little boy in hotel uniform is a "plant." He goes in in the uniform for the few minutes it takes for you to come down in the lift, takes your bet and your money and goes straight out and gives it to our friend on the telephone and is untraceable from there on in! Of course you have to work it on sentimental mugs but apparently he was doing a great line of business with English actresses. Maybe he was just a frustrated actor who enjoyed playing the role of an Englishman and found it more profitable off stage than on!

So six weeks in New York ended rather sadly although it is a fantastic city. It is a city of success. Failure is not within its ken. Failure is catching and must be avoided just as success is all that matters and must be cultivated at all costs. It must be an incredible experience to be the toast of New York because it's a bandwagon on to which everyone climbs. But alack and alas we sneaked out with our flags at half-mast and hardly a soul to wish us goodbye. I lost a stone in weight and went back bewitched by all that I had seen of New York bemused by not only having been conned into losing my money, but having had all my jewellery, what little I had, stolen the night before we left, and bewildered, by the speed at which one can be a star one minute and a nothing the next. Jacques' open arms were never more welcome than on my return.

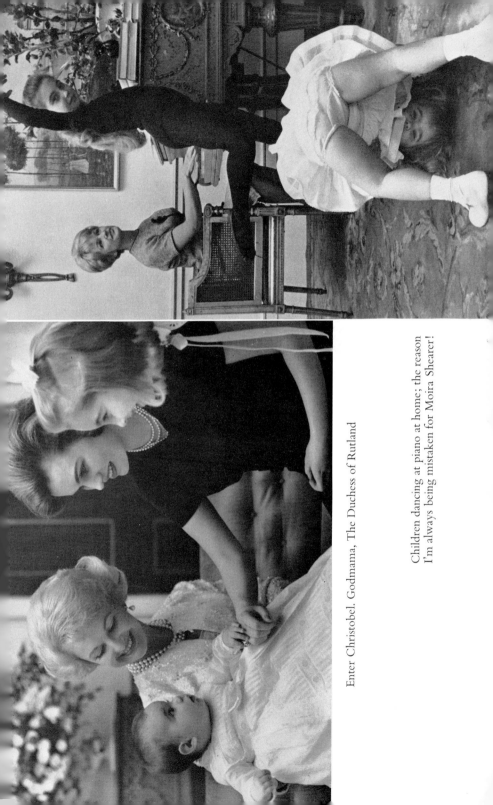

Enter Christobel. Godmama, The Duchess of Rutland

Children dancing at piano at home; the reason
I'm always being mistaken for Moira Shearer!

Bob Hope: "Shall I kiss you now or shall I tease you a little first?"

Rex Harrison – Sexy Rexy, can't vouch for it personally – never really had the chance!

Chapter 11

Y cycle of bad luck was to dog me a little while
longer. But I do believe one learns far more from
failure than from success. I was asked to do a revue.
I leapt at the chance. I adore music, love the changing of parts
so many times in an evening and I was to star with a wonderful
cast, all of whom have now become famous. Norman Wisdom,
Tommy Cooper, Muriel Smith, Bob Monkhouse and Buddy
Bradley, who was doing the choreography, and Audrey
Hepburn, who was in the chorus as a dancer. It was a great
spectacular with all the glamour of a Palladium show. It was
thought nothing of having real rain as a backing to a song. A
revolving stage, everything was there for the asking. It cost a
fortune. But it was one of the unhappiest shows I've ever been
in. Everyone was unhappy, the atmosphere was thick with
discontent. Everyone seemed to have something to upset
them. I, for one, had violent hysteria (something I had never
experienced before or since) ten minutes before curtain-up.
And I had to do a Yoga on myself, trying to convince myself
that this was not me Moira Lister the person going on but
Moira Lister the actress, and I actually achieved a sort of coming out of my own body and detached myself from what was
going on.

I can hardly remember doing the opening chorus with my
body trembling so much that I had to dig my nails into my
partner to stop myself passing out. How I got through that
opening night I shall never know. The notices were bad the
next day although fortunately I personally came out very well.
But we knew we were doomed. We struggled through and

mercifully closed after six weeks. After the first week, little Audrey Hepburn's only solo number with Norman Wisdom was thrown out on the assumption that neither of them were good enough. That was a pretty pathetic conclusion in view of their subsequent and warranted present status. Also she was in love with Marcel le Bon, a beautiful French singer who must have been out of his mind not to return her affection, and she spent her twenty-first birthday in my dressing room in tears bemoaning the fact that although she was under contract to A.B.C. she was not being properly handled, that she felt she was a failure because she wasn't given the breaks and was still a chorus girl at twenty-one, and that Marcel was ignoring her. She wanted to give the whole thing up. I tried to comfort her as best I could, telling her that even in the chorus one couldn't look at anyone else, which was absolutely true. She had a magnetism which was infinitely compelling. I knew she was loaded with talent and I was certainly not the only one, because not very long after that Colette, the author of *Gigi*, saw her sitting in a bistro and offered her the title part on Broadway and from that moment she has never looked back.

Well, my rule of three was about to prove itself. Two bad breaks and one to go. But of the last one I was unconsolable. I went to Paris to star with François Perrier in *Mon Phoque et Elle*. I was loving every minute of the film, speaking in French of which I was now very proud. Cavorting around the studios with a real live seal and having the greatest fun, but in the middle of it all I had a cable to say my beloved mother, whom I knew was on the way from South Africa to come and stay with me in London, had been taken off the boat at Southampton by doctors and was very ill indeed. I got leave from the film to fly home and there was my beautiful little mother lying in bed in great, great pain. I sent for doctors immediately and they confirmed our worst fears. It was galloping cancer. She had never had a day's illness in her life, and always said don't let them take me to hospital because I know I'll never come back.

I promised to keep her at home. Of course she had no idea what was wrong with her. And when the four men came with a huge portable X-ray machine because she was too ill to be moved, she took one look at them and smiled and said, "My, you look grim, all of you, how about something to cheer you up – what would you like – Bryon, Keats, Shelley or Shakespeare. Shakespeare? Right. Here goes." And she launched into the entire Battle of Agincourt speech from *Henry V* without a single mistake, then as an encore she took my hand in hers and in a manner of pure inspiration recited Shakespeare's sonnet which runs:

> *"When forty winters shall besiege thy brow*
> *And dig deep trenches in thy beauty's field,*
> *Thy youth's proud livery, so gaz'd on now,*
> *Will be a tatter'd weed, of small worth held.*
> *Then being asked where all thy beauty lies,*
> *Where all the treasure of thy lusty days,*
> *To say, within thine own deep-sunken eyes,*
> *Were an all-eating shame and thriftless praise.*
> *How much more praise deserv'd thy beauty's use,*
> *If thy could'st answer – This fair child of mine,*
> *Shall sum my count, and make my old excuse,*
> *Proving her beauty by succession thine!*
> *This were to be new-made when thou art old*
> *And see thy blood warm when thou feel'st it cold."*

Well, far from cheering us up tears were streaming down the faces of the four men, to say nothing of my own. She laughed and said we all looked as though we were going to a funeral. Poor darling didn't know how near the truth she was. I moved her bed down into the drawing room so she could see out into the Square. It was May and the pink and white blossoms were out. I couldn't leave her side and it broke my heart to see her deteriorating so rapidly. Finally, after only two weeks the doctor insisted she be taken to a nursing home because she would have to be under heavy sedation to ease the pain. I arranged for a large Daimler with a bed in the back of it so she would not know she was going in an ambulance. Only once in the nursing home did she recognise me – but just squeezed my hand, smiled and went off to sleep happy that my sisters and I were there. That was the last I saw of her. She died shortly afterwards. I think a part of me died with her. I loved her with a deep devotion and today, eighteen years later, I still feel her presence so strongly that she could almost be in the room. I dream of her on an average three times a week even now. She was the ideal of what every mother should be, warm, understanding, generous to a fault, talented, beautiful and witty, the greatest fun to be with yet commanding the best kind of respect. Just a queen among women. I pray I will be the same to my children but I am afraid the standards set by her were so high that I could at best only be a very poor second.

I went back to Paris to finish the film a very changed person – nothing meant anything to me. It took me all my strength to assume the gay role I was portraying. That is one of the tough parts of this job, that your heart can be breaking and yet the smile has to come at command.

I returned to England after the burial which mercifully I was spared. I have no idea where she is buried and asked expressly not to be told because I was incapable of accepting the fact that that little delicate porcelain body was under six feet of earth. Gradually with the pressure of work and time I adapted myself to the fact that life had to be lived without her and tried to fill the gap with more and more activity. Happily I got a marvellous role starring opposite Tyrone Power in *Seven Waves Away* and was able to devote myself to that. Dear Tyrone Power, much more devastating off screen than on, and as charming as he was handsome. The whole film took eight weeks, which were spent in a tank at Shepperton. The story took place in a lifeboat. But however strong the story of the film was, the real life drama on the boat was even more interesting to observe. It was the first time I have seen a love affair disintegrate through sheer geography. There were about fifteen of us in the boat. Tyrone Power and Mai Zetterling were in the prow facing the rest of us. I was in the second row and behind me was a girl called Jill Melford who was, when the picture started, "walking out" with Ty. In the beginning loving looks were shooting over my head to her and the unspoken words found their way across the boat right into her lap. But gradually, I suppose because of chemistry and maybe propinquity, Mai Zetterling's presence began to make itself felt. A foot would go on Ty's foot, a hand would rest just that minute longer than necessary, and soon the looks above my head began to lessen and to turn in Mai's direction, and by the end of the picture Jill had lost her love and Mai had gained the prize. I can't help feeling that if only the seating accommodation in the lifeboat had been different it all might never have happened. But as I believe so implicitly in the balance of life; one loses one thing and gains another. Jill is now happily married to John Standing, a marvellous person and a super actor. She is star of a howling success with Donald Sinden called *Not Now Darling*. She has a gorgeous son, and Kay Hammond as a mum-in-law – so I suppose fate knows what it's doing.

While we were on the picture my sister Evelyn, who lives in Tasmania and has always had a very protective instinct towards me, visited me on the set. Now it happened that after having been in the freezing water for two hours at a stretch the studio would give us a tot of brandy to revive us. My sister arrived at ten-thirty a.m. just as I was leaving the tank after a two hour soak, and as I greeted her my dresser came up to me and said, "Your brandy, Miss Lister." My sister was horrified, checked the time, ten-thirty a.m. on her watch, turned to me and said, "And when did *this* start?"

Seven Waves Away was the penultimate picture Ty did before he died. He was, strangely enough, a believer in the now notorious cult of Scientology. He told me that he would never die of a disease because he would never allow disease to enter his body. That he was capable of building enough defence mechanism to fight off any germ that might attack him through sheer control of his body through his mind. It was strange that he died of heart failure not long after.

Chapter 12

Now was the time for Peter Ustinov to burst into my life.

I first met Ustinov at Pinewood Studios in 1947 while making a picture with Dirk Bogarde called *Once A Jolly Swagman*. I was sitting in the restaurant and a large cuddly bear was suddenly there before me, asking me if he could see me again to discuss a new play he had written. He was by then the young intellectual genius of the day. I was flattered and delighted.

The following week we met and he talked in relentless detail of the play *The Trojan Women* and of the role of Helen of Troy he wanted me to play. His descriptions were so compelling that the entire battle took place before my eyes. I couldn't wait to read the play. I was at the time starring opposite Noel Coward in *Present Laughter*. I read it and unhappily, because of my youth, ignorance and impertinence, turned down the play. Obviously my mind was not developed enough to assimilate it. It was, in fact, way above my head. That was the end of a beautiful friendship for two years. But as his largesse was not only physical, he had the grace to offer me what has probably been the most rewarding role of my career, in the *Love of Four Colonels*.

Well, to spend two years in bed as Peter Ustinov's Sleeping Beauty is a pretty traumatic experience for any young actress! Each day gave birth to a new character in Peter's endless gamut. I would wait each evening for him to come into my dressing room, wondering "who" he was going to be for my amusement that particular night. Depending where he had been and whom he had seen during the day, so would he relate to me, with all the embellishments, the tapestry of characters he had absorbed. I would be a sort of testing ground for the characterisations, epigrams, situations, which were jelling in his brain, to be fashioned and refined into the lives of his plays and the performances of his great personality. Then he would go to his dressing room and while putting on his make-up and during each break of the play, he would be jotting down scenes of plays, ideas, studies, always accompanied by his own inimitable cartoons which are slightly reminiscent of Scarfe.

His brain has such an abnormal capacity of retention. He would read great tomes of Roman History and unbelievingly I would open the book at around page two thousand and ask him about the characters (which I had hurriedly cribbed up). He would repeat almost verbatim their descriptions.

When *The Colonels* opened on tour in Birmingham, it ran almost four hours and the audience stood up and cheered. The Management descended in force and told him to cut an hour and a half out of the play. His reply was, "Why? *Hamlet* runs four hours and this is funnier." However, they insisted and my heart bled as pages of scintillating dialogue and thought ended in the waste-paper basket. If only I'd had the presence of mind to collect it.

We opened at Wyndham's and the town flocked. It was terribly exciting, but more exciting was working with Peter. It was like setting off a new Roman Candle every night. One night during the Chekovian scene, he decided it would be fun to be pestered by an imaginary bee – it was hilarious, the audience adored it and I, alas, collapsed in hysterical laughter into his lap and he had to finish the scene alone.

On matinée days, we had the usual trouble with tea-trays, which we hated, especially during the American sequence. Whenever he shot the gun, the old ladies would get such a start their trays would shoot off their knees, with a consequent crash of china. One particular afternoon, he went *on* shooting the gun, so that every tray shot off every lap and we had peace for the rest of the afternoon.

During the time that Sir Alec Guinness was playing Hamlet at the next-door theatre, two Americans came in to see our play and after the first act went to the box office demanding their money back, saying they had never seen such a travesty of a play, it was a disgrace, etc., etc. The management went to Peter, very distressed, and asked him what to do. Peter said immediately, "Give them their money back by all means," and as the manager gave Peter the two tickets, he noticed they were two seats for *Hamlet*!

Then there were the unique after-theatre parties at Peter's home or mine, where we would invite our chums and Peter would sit for hours doing his musical impersonations, recounting anecdotes, sending up his audience. Theodore Bikel would play the guitar and sing songs of the Kibutz, and I would fill in the empty spaces with whatever I could.

Peter's such a chameleon that he can enter into the skin of almost any character to such an extent that when he was playing Nero, in America, he was so convincing that he was fêted by the gullible film world as a veritable Caesar. "Alas, poor Yorick" when he played a slave in the next film, he was shunned by the same public, who were convinced that Ustinov was "on the skids".

One of the most enchanting stories Peter told me, when we were in Ireland for the opening of *Photo Finish*, was that one day he was driving down Grafton Street, when a woman walked off the pavement, held up her hand for him to stop his car and proceeded to put a wreath on the road in front of it. Peter, mystified, got out and asked her the reason for her strange gesture. She explained that her husband had been killed in a motor-car smash on that very spot and that the wreath was to commemorate the first anniversary of his death.

Peter's wit has always been so sharp and his observations so graphic, that every time he writes a play a *chef-d'oeuvre* is always expected of him. This, he has told me, disturbs him, as he feels he too should be allowed to write for the public and not only for the critics. Personally, being in tremendous awe of his unique gifts, I find anything he writes is unclichéd, stimulating, witty and never lacking in depth, and I feel very grateful and humble that he should have considered me adequate enough to have allowed me to create one of his roles.

And the Sleeping Beauty was one of the most satisfying roles I have ever played. Apart from being the ideal of four different colonels, a Russian, an American, a French and an English, each scene was the incarnation of their environment, so for an actress it meant a Chekov character, a gangster's moll, a Molière and a Shakespearean character. I had five wigs because there was also the Sleeping Beauty, and five super costumes and it was stimulating to play the five different roles. At a party one night a rather grand lady came up to me and said, "They tell me you are an actress, are you giving anything at the moment?" I explained I was in the *Love of Four Colonels*. "Ah," she said, "I've seen that. Now what part do you play?" I swallowed that one and said, "The Sleeping Beauty." "Oh well," she said, "you don't have very much to do just lying in bed all evening, do you?" Politely I swallowed that one too, and said, "I do actually play the other four parts as well!" "Oh," she said, "That is most intriguing. I kept saying to my husband, I wonder who all these pretty gals are that keep coming on!" She obviously had not understood one word of the play from beginning to end!

When I went to get my shoes for the American role I was told to get the highest pair of patent leather I could find. I was told of a shop in Shaftesbury Avenue that sold shoes for ladies of the "other" profession. I sailed in gaily and made my request. Out came a pair of patent shoes with twelve-inch heels. I tried them on and practically fell over. I said to the assistant, "But I can't walk in these." His reply was, "But, Madame, these shoes are not for *walking* in!" I took the next height down and fled!

After the play had been running a year, I thought it was time for the addition of a fifth colonel! And so finally, after far too many years of vacillation, Jacques and I decided to get married. By this time Jacques had gone into the champagne world and was feeling more flush about the future and I was beginning to feel the temptation of too much attention from the gentlemen of the town. I was being pursued by the good-time boys with coronets and the handsome actors without. Probably I should have kept my message block on the memorable day I had the grand coup of being telephoned by one prince, one actor, two dukes, one director, an earl, an extrovert, and my own Vicomte! But weighing them all up, their distinguished names, their fortunes and their various good looks, I plumbed for the one who had the least money, and since the Revolution the lesser title, but the best nature and undoubtedly the most fun to live with. So as I had a weekend off at Christmas-time in the December of 1951 we flew off to Paris after we had been married in a chapel adjacent to the grounds now owned by Paul Getty at Sutton Place.

To me a wedding is a very private experience. I wanted to be completely alone in the church with my husband-to-be so the ceremony would have its full value, which after all is the union of two people in the sight of God. So all I had was the minimum requirement, a best man and a matron of honour. My school girl-friend from South Africa, who also happened to have married a French nobleman, the Comte de Renty, came with her husband from Paris, and that was all. I had no family here and neither did Jacques. I was married in a white lace shortie wedding dress (very "with it" at the time!), a short white veil and a white fox coat as it was in the depths of winter. We were married at eight a.m. in the morning and the only public who assisted the wedding were fifty photographers who had somehow got wind of the event. We left immediately for Paris for a forty-eight hour honeymoon. After all this time, six years since I had first met Jacques, suddenly in the space of forty-eight hours I was a real live Vicomtesse, with a very strange name that it took me quite some time to get used to let alone spell. I was now Madame Gachassin-Lafite, Vicomtesse d' Orthez. I went away quietly in a corner and practised spelling it. It was a title which had been created in 1555 and of which Jacques was not unduly proud. He spent hours trying to enlighten me as to its glorious and inglorious history.

From the first family in 1140, the Comte de Foix who were the Seigneurs of Orthez, to the letters of patent from the Queen of Navarre, Henry IV's mother, incorporating the Gachassin and creating the title of Vicomte d'Orthez; through the Revolution, the Battle of Orthez, 1815, in which Wellington had thirty-two British regiments fighting there, and down to the lands owned by Jacques' grandfather and subsequently given to the church where Bernadette had her visitation. All this was like a picture history book to me, something interesting but very remote from me. What mattered to me was the man I had married, not his background or his name. These were just bonuses. So it was with comparative ease that I was able to pick up my role in the *Love of Four Colonels* where I was to stay until the end of my second year.

After two years Peter became restless and wanted to go. So as we only had six weeks left, Clifford Mollison took over. His nickname was "Stiffy" Mollison and I was to discover why on his opening night. Playing the wicked fairy Clifford had to, what we call, "underdress", to save time with the changes. So several layers of costume were put over each other. Of course the basic costume had to be the gaily striped tights which he wore for the Elizabethan scene. But in his nervousness of his opening night he got the layers a bit mixed and when he made his entrance behind me on the rostrum I heard four colonels who were in the Proscenium boxes, hoot with stifled laughter. I couldn't think what had happened until I looked back to find that poor Clifford had made his entrance with his "jock-strap" *over* his tights instead of *under*. I couldn't utter for the next five minutes during which the boys in the box were taking bets as to whether Clifford was really that interesting shape or whether slight additions had been made to impress the public. Anyway, he was a dear man and we all loved him.

So two momentous years of my life ended with the closing of *The Colonels*. I don't think I have enjoyed a play quite so much since.

It was during this time that we bought the large house in Hans Place. One day I will write a book on "How to Remain a Lady while keeping Lodgers!" After we had finished decorating it we discovered we were working simply to keep the house going. It swallowed every penny we earned, so I had to make a flat at the top in order to help pay the rent. Then I needed a couple to run the place so I went to the Italian convent in London and they sent me a couple. They were not actually married but couldn't live without each other, or more precisely he couldn't live without the work she did! She was a fabulous cook but only under his guidance. He had been, so he told me, a veterinary surgeon in Naples and she was a couturier by profession, but they were quite prepared to work as butler and cook. After a few weeks they asked if they could go to a school to learn English. I agreed, and after they had been attending for about three weeks I was sitting in the library, past which the basement steps went, and I noticed a beautifully dressed, if rather thin, lady go down the steps, ring their bell and go in. I was interested as I didn't think they knew anyone in England. She stayed half an hour then left, and within five minutes another extremely elegant lady, again rather thin, went down, rang the bell and went in. Now I became disturbed. What was going on in the basement? I didn't want to interrupt anything so decided the moment she left to go down. However, as she left she was crossed on the steps by yet a third elegant lady. Pacing up and down in my library, I had the grace to wait twenty minutes, then I rang the bell. Rita came up flushed and upset. "Where is Emelio?" "He busy," she said with tears in her eyes. "Tell him to come here immediately." I braced myself to attack him on his below-stairs activities. He came into the room almost surprised that he had been summoned. "What, might I ask, do you think you are doing downstairs?" "I do a very good job. These ladies I meet at English school, come to me because they gotta very little breasts. I have very gooda serum from Italy. I inject – I massage – and pouf they gotta lovely bigga breasts!" And this from a veterinary surgeon! I explained very plainly that this was not allowed in England and he must stop immediately. "Pity," he said. "Very easy money, can give you some if you like." That would have gone down well in the press. I firmly closed the subject. No hard feelings – just a pity!

Our next episode was letting the flat upstairs. I was away when two dapper young men in Savile Row suits arrived. Delighted with the flat they paid one month in advance and told Emelio to ring up Fortnums and fill it with flowers, fruit and *fois gras*. Incidentally they told Emelio not to disturb them during the day as they slept late and not to worry if they were late coming home. They signed on as Mr. Rich and Mr. Steele. One week later the C.I.D. came to the door and asked if we had a Mr. Royce and Mr. Stannard staying in the house. No, we said. Then they brought out pictures of our two dapper young men. We had to admit they had taken the flat. The C.I.D. men went straight upstairs to await their return, explaining that they were two of the most dangerous cat burglars in London. And when they came back the handcuffs were smartly snapped on them, and they were taken away. One got seven years, the other five. Probably they would have got more because when we cleaned out the flat we found a loaded revolver down the side of each chair in which they had been sitting. But I couldn't help admiring their wit signing in as Mr. Rich and Mr. Steele!

The next tenant in the flat was a rather faded middle-aged woman who described herself as a corsetier. She was also delighted with the flat and paid half the rent and said she would pay the balance when her friend whom she was expecting left. She explained that she had been in France and that I mustn't mind if she had a lot of phone calls because she had put an advertisement in Shepherd Market (naïve as I was it didn't click even then) that she was back in business. Indeed, next day the telephone rang incessantly and by six p.m. there was a queue of bowler-hatted and umbrella'd men waiting outside the front door. I, thinking they were all in the corset trade, asked them to wait in the hall. It was only when I saw another rather sleezy-looking woman go up did it dawn on me that maybe things were not all they seemed. I determined to intercept the next phone call which went something like this:

Man: "I saw your advertisement. What price do you charge?"
Woman: "Three guineas and five guineas."
Man: "What do you do for three guineas and what for five?"
Woman: "I never describe details on the phone, but if you're looking for someone young and pretty, that's not me, but if you want someone warm and understanding and who knows all the tricks of the trade, then that's me!"
Man: "Good, when can you see me?"
Woman: "I have a very full schedule but seven-fifteen will be convenient."
Man: "I'll be there."

Horrified I dropped the phone, my mind boggling at what must be going on in my beautiful flat upstairs. I turned all the men out of the hall – hadn't the courage to go up myself so sent Emilio to give her one hour to get out or else I'd fetch the police. I thought for a moment Emilio might leave with her, then I remembered she had a big bust so there would be no point!

To crown everything my little Irish maid who had the face of an angel and looked sixteen, plump and fresh and lovely, gave birth to an illegitimate baby in the basement. Jacques, who was alone in the house – I was out rehearsing – had to do the honours, a pretty messy job as she was fully clothed when it happened and it arrived in exactly five minutes. He in a frenzy rang the ambulance. They came with a midwife who mistook Jacques for the father, and after she had efficiently done her job, went straight to Jacques and said, "I'm sure you'll be pleased to know, sir, that mother and child have been separated – you have a lovely little girl." With which Jacques went straight to the brandy bottle and was snow-white and stoned by the time I got back.

So the saga of the house went on and on, till finally we decided that the whole thing was far too much for us to cope with, so let it for ten years fully furnished to one of the lesser Embassies. After one year they did a bunk, taking part of our furniture with them to furnish their new abode. I fought the case for two years, and finally gave up and on a claim of sixteen-thousand pounds settled for two-thousand five hundred and they simply claimed diplomatic immunity for the rest. We sold the house a year later and moved into Cadogan Square where we still are, in what *Look* magazine described as a "stunning duplex".

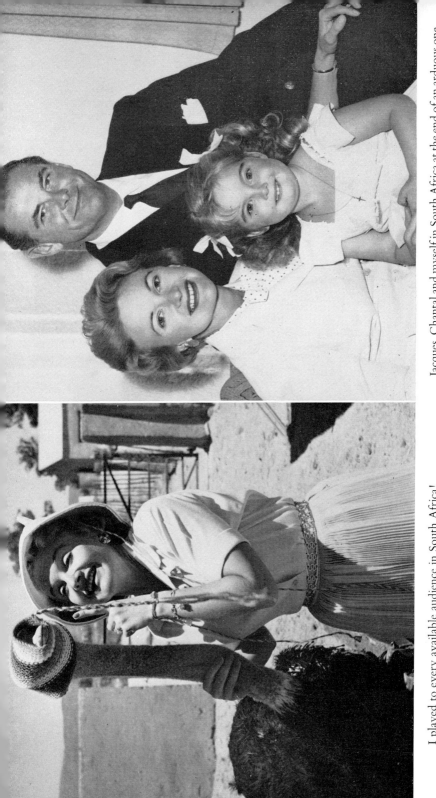

I played to every available audience in South Africa!

Jacques, Chantal and myself in South Africa at the end of an arduous one woman show tour of 75,000 miles, finishing in Australia

My orchestral debut at the Albert Hall – four notes as a nightingale! *Back row:* Edmundo Ros, Lord Boothby, Cliff Michelmore, Len Hutton. *Seated:* Katie Boyle, Moira Lister, Margaret Rutherford

Chapter 13

WHEN the play came to an end I was badly in need of a holiday and after the first year of marriage, which is the difficult adjusting period where sensitivities are at their most vulnerable, I felt I needed to go away into the mountains and let all the twisted knots unravel so I could return relaxed and ready to attack another demanding year.

So alone I went off to my little resort that had done me so much good before, Crans-sur-Sierre. But this time I wasn't running away from anything. I was just exhausted and needed rest.

I think the first three days I simply slept. At night in my bed, by day on the balcony in the sun. Occasionally I would open my eyes and drink in the staggering sight of the mountains covered in what looked like great wadges of whipped cream. The pine trees heavy with the night's fall of snow, the sun blazing from a brilliant blue sky, and in the distance sleigh bells and a sort of beehive buzz of children's voices as they whisked down the slopes. Soon I was feeling a tingling in my toes which was the first sign of life returning to me. And it wasn't long before that manifested itself into skis, boots, jerseys, anorak and off! But it seems I am never able just to do things in a nice ordinary humdrum way like everyone else. No. Something always seems to have to happen to me. This time was no exception.

I had been ski-ing all day and was pretty tired. I had done the run with a very nice man who invited me to take a glass of wine with him when we got back to the hotel. Happily for me I accepted, otherwise I would not be here to tell the tale. It was five p.m. and getting dark. We were the last ones up the mountain, and I was too tired to ski down again, so I insisted he ski down and I would take the last automatic funicular. He agreed and off he went. I climbed into the little cable car for four all alone and started to descend. About a third of the way down it suddenly stopped with a nasty jerk. I looked down and the car was hanging thousands of feet high from a thin piece of cable. I quickly sat down again, quite sure it was just a temporary stop. It wasn't. The minutes started to slip by. The wind began to sway the little car from one side to another. The sun had gone and the dark was beginning to envelop the mountains all round. Now my heart started to race. I realised they'd switched the motor off not knowing there was anyone in the car and had gone home. I began to shiver. I could no longer feel my hands or feet. What could I do? How long could I stand the intense cold before I died of exposure? The wind grew stronger, the car rocked more wildly and more precariously and I grew colder. I started to panic. I must get out, I can't die here alone, there must be a safety device of some kind. There was a rope. I got it down and unwound it and let it go over the side of the window. It looked like a little piece of string dangling uselessly over a vast abyss underneath. Furious I threw it away. I put up the window. It was now getting near freezing point, but I was frightened to jump or move too much in case too much movement unhooked the car from its delicate position and it would either crash to the bottom or go hurtling down the cable to smash to smithereens and me with it into the cable house below.

I was sobbing with terror, cold and the senseless futility of it all. The minutes slipped into hours. Two at least had passed and it was now pitch-dark. I could see the lights in the village miles below. I was quite frantic by now. I started to pray, and pray furiously at great speed, and somewhere in my brain I was hatching a plan to jump. The thought of dying slowly and alone up there was abhorrent to me. I would rather end it quickly. I stood up and could hardly keep my balance as the car was swaying so much. I put my hand on the window but because my hand was frozen I didn't have the strength to open it. My God, now I really was in a coffin, and sank on to my knees and let myself cry out, pleading with God to help me. In fact, I was making so much noise that I hardly noticed that the car had started to move. I couldn't believe it. But it was true, slowly and surely I was being taken back to life.

What had happened was that my friend had gone back to the hotel, found I wasn't there, waited an hour, called my room, then realised I hadn't returned, went to the cable house, found everyone had gone home, had looked up the mountain and had seen the tiny red speck of car near the top of the mountain. Had got the guard away from his evening meal – with difficulty – and insisted they see if I was in the car. And I was or what was left of me! I was never happier to get back home and into the warm arms of my husband than after that trip.

The next two years passed fairly uneventfully, and then of all the emotions I had experienced throughout my twenty-nine years now was to come the one that had the profoundest effect on me.

I was starring in a play at the Criterion called *Birthday Honours*. We had been open just one month. It was not a wild success but we were holding our own. Balmain had made a fabulous wardrobe for me for the play and I was having to watch every mouthful of food in case I started to bulge in the wrong places. One Saturday matinée I felt terribly ill and didn't think I could play the evening show. This for me was catastrophe because I'd never missed a performance in my life. Marion Spencer who was playing my mother wasn't well either so I assumed we had caught a bug of some kind. I sent for my doctor to come to the theatre between the shows. I explained my symptoms and he examined me and within a very short while informed me that I was pregnant. Sick as I was I was out of my mind with joy. It gave me the strength to go on for the evening performance. I struggled through feeling worse every minute until just about ten minutes before the curtain was due to come down I started haemorrhaging very badly. Fortunately I was wearing a long dress. I couldn't leave the stage so stuck it till curtain down, was helped to my dressing room and passed out. And fortunately nobody in the theatre knew why. When I recovered I got a taxi, went home and rang the doctor to tell him what had happened. He said it probably meant that I had lost the baby or would lose it shortly, that I was to go to bed and stay there for two weeks and not put my feet to the ground.

When I told Jacques about the baby and saw the black look on his face I realised for the first time that he really didn't want children. It was a kind of possessiveness about me. He loved me and was afraid children would come between us. I tried to convince him that I would love him more because of our child, but I drew a blank. This attitude didn't help my condition much. I stayed in bed the whole weekend and on the Monday morning had to ring the theatre to say I would not be playing that night. Now as the play had only been running a month I didn't want to let the management down by telling them I was pregnant. Anyway, I didn't know if I still was. So I simply said I had gastric enteritis, and the doctor thought I would be back in ten days. The reply came back that Marion Spencer had gastric enteritis and as we only had one understudy between us, she was already on, and I wasn't covered. "What do we do in a case like this?" I asked. "Well, we will have to send someone on with a book to read your part." I was in a terrible spot. I thought of all those people paying their money to see an understudy reading the leading part. The pro in me turned upside down and without thinking I said I'll come down tonight. Well, I played the whole fortnight and how I did I'll never know. Tots of brandy were placed in key positions on the stage which I had to sip surreptitiously when I felt I was going to faint. It was a nightmare, but the audience probably didn't notice much difference. By some miracle at the end of six weeks the test came back to say I still had my baby with me. And in fact we acted nightly together in *Birthday Honours* for five whole months. By which time I was just beginning to have to let the seams out of my Balmain's. I could have gone on longer only dear Bill Boorne, whom I still love in spite of the quickness of his pen, published my secret in the *Evening News*. The management were horrified and very disbelieving, but once the story was out, it wasn't very nice for the role I was playing of a doctor's wife with a couple of lovers thrown in to be played by a pregnant actress! So I was sacked! I was really rather relieved as it had been a great strain hiding it from everyone. Now I could relax and grow fat.

As the subject of the baby was never mentioned at home, which grieved me greatly, I decided to go away by myself. I went to Majorca for the last three months, and stayed in a little hotel where I just swam and lay all day in the sun. Also I bought the famous Grantly Dick Read book on natural child-birth. I studied this avidly – practised all the relaxed breathing and did all the exercises, and firmly believed I was going to be delivered without any pain at all. Jacques came out and fetched me ten days before the baby was due. The ten days passed plus another ten. Nothing happened. So they put me in the nursing home for induction. Two more days, nothing happened. I went in again and at last labour started with a vengeance. Now I brought all my lessons to the fore – every time I had a pain I breathed deeply and tried to relax. Actually it made no difference at all; the pain was still excruciating. But determined not to be outdone I worked at it even harder. During this the matron came in, looked at me and walked straight out. The sister on duty asked her how I was. "Oh, she's all right, she's an actress, we'll soon know when she's in pain!"

When the actual birth came all my good work went for nothing. I had to be "put out" as there were complications. They had to use instruments, anyway. And when I came round from the anaesthetic I was so furious at having been let down in my faith that it was all going to be painless that the first words I said were, not something moving like "Is it a girl or is it a boy?" but very forcibly, "Bugger Grantly Dick Read!"

However, that was all very soon forgotten when they put that baby into my arms for the first time; a complete metamorphosis took place in me. I had become a mother and it was an extraordinary sensation. I had at last created something real and tangible. And of all my productions, this one surpassed the lot. She was not a particularly pretty baby, in fact when Jacques first saw her, he said, "My God, it's Giles' grandmother!" And he wasn't far wrong, but to me she was the most fabulous baby in the world. And from that moment I began to see "people" differently. I became more tolerant, warmer, in fact more human. I had lived so long in the make-believe world of theatre that reality was in danger of becoming submerged. But now here was what life is all about. This little seven-pound bundle of nothingness. Yet the whole world seemed to begin and end with it.

When I took her home I wanted only the best for her. The most beautiful room, the most beautiful clothes, the most glamorous godparents, and there my dukes and princes came in handy. I wanted her to be a princess because to me she was. However, the best-laid plans go astray, and when she was christened by an eighty-year-old bishop with a bevy of illustrious and since proved wonderful godparents, the name Chantal was a bit too much for the bishop who very determinedly christened her Chanel, to which everyone under their breaths answered No. 5!!

She grew more beautiful every day but it was six weeks later that I noticed her little head was always on one side. My maternity sister confirmed my observations and we discovered she had one muscle shorter than the other on the neck. I took her to the best paediatrician in London and he told me that every day for one year I would have to give her exercises to stretch that muscle. These exercises involved lifting her by her head, hanging her upside down by the feet and forcing the head from one side to the other. Of course they caused pain, and there were tears every time. I was desperate lest she could associate me with pain, but the doctors assured me this was not so. And they were right. Finally she was absolutely cured and still seemed to love me as much as I loved her.

When she was about eight months old I had an offer to star with Sir John Gielgud, Dame Peggy Ashcroft and George Devine, in a European tour plus London season of *Much Ado* and *King Lear*. I only accepted as I would not be away from home more than four weeks during the year that we played.

It was a great year. We were the first English company to play the capital cities of Europe since the war. In Germany we played West Berlin. But to get there had to land in East Berlin and climbed on a bus with guards with loaded sten-guns at the door. The Russians had not yet left Vienna. So the whole atmosphere was fascinating. I was asked by the London *Daily Mail* to write a series of articles on the tour. Here are a few extracts of the interesting places, written in my best journalese!

VIENNA

"The sharp, shrill scream of the turbo-jet Viscount's lightning take-off 350 miles per hour up through the strato-cumulus (a rather grand term for cloud) into the sun and nearer to heaven, and we were on our way to Vienna, on the first lap of our European Shakespearian tour to the striped green velvet lands of Austria and, to our great surprise, plump into the Russian zone, in the heart of which lies the airport of Vienna.

"What a contrast! Primitive, sad, bombed, and with a feeling of being deeply behind the Iron Curtain.

"Into the beautiful city of Vienna, full of atmosphere, of past glories and beauties, and steeped in antiquity.

"Our first play *Much Ado About Nothing* was an enormous

success – with a wildly enthusiastic audience – they practically all turned up at the stage door afterwards and continued the applause there.

"A slight difference between the Austrian teenage autograph hunters and others I have met was not to ask for personal dedications but for a quotation from the play.

"Sir Geoffrey Wallinger gave a most sumptuous party for us at the newly renovated-after-bombing British Embassy.

"The buffet seemed inexhaustible; pride of place went to whole suckling pigs, carved and served by a most distinguished-looking chef.

"A string orchestra played predominantly Viennese waltzes. What joy to dance them with the men here, who take their intricacies as seriously as we take cricket. Noblemen abounded with charm and grace and wit. I upbraided one for not remembering the colour of a girl's dress when he was talking about her in exuberant terms. He said, 'Aber, Madame, we Austrians would remember the colour of a woman's eyes, her hair, the shape of her figure and the touch of her skin – but never the colour of her dress!'

"I had a long chat with the Russian Ambassador on Shakespeare versus Chekov. I thought that was safe enough ground. He graciously let Shakespeare win . . .

"Before I leave Vienna I must tell you that it is here in this city that I have experienced one of the greatest moments in my life – a moment which takes you out of time and space and sends you for a while into eternity.

"In the Emperor's private chapel I assisted at the Mozart High Mass, sung by the Vienna Boys' Choir and played by the Philharmonic Orchestra.

"Here my descriptive powers fall sadly short, because I cannot describe to you how great it was to have the notes of the orchestra ringing out into the architraves, the purity of the boys' voices, and the sublimity of Mozart's music, all merged together with the sacrifice of the Mass.

"It was almost too beautiful to bear and was an experience I shall never forget."

ZÜRICH

"We are back on the plane, sailing forth into a threatening sky as we leave Vienna, with its many palaces and churches looking like exquisite tiny toys, over Schönbrunn, the miniature Versailles, the silver ribbon of the Danube, and lastly the Vienna woods, to conquer new horizons and bring the Stratford Memorial Theatre into the Schauspielhaus of Zürich.

"Halfway out we hit a bad storm. I looked round and saw the happy, smiling faces gradually turn from pink to puce, to pale pea green. Lunches were refused, seat belts fastened as the heavens opened to drop us and several thousand tons of water on Zürich at the same time.

"But to us the sun shone again soon. For as we landed safely we were welcomed with a rose each and a charming silk handkerchief. On it is printed a map of Zürich, which I am using for the sole purpose of finding my way around.

"Zürich is the richest city in Europe, where everything exudes at once opulence, industry, thrift and prosperity; where directors start work at 7 a.m., schools at 7.30, where even a working-class boy must be the proud possessor of £500 before he dares venture for the hand of his beloved.

"But for all that the aesthetic side of her nature is not lacking. We were received by the city fathers in the room where Goethe first translated Shakespeare, where at the age of ten Mozart gave his first concert.

"Wagner, too, whose house overlooks the lake, translated darker and more turbulent moods into musical literature . . .

"Each week has had a moment of magic, but our last day in Zürich was a whole magical day. Awakened by a brilliant sun, breakfast on the terrace, and a short, sharp dip in the lake. Then into a high-powered car and off into the mountains, through picture-postcard villages, with the mysteriously black Black

Forest on the horizon, and in the valley the swift torrent of the Rhine.

"On to the rather terrifying but glorious Rhine-fall, where the Rhine literally 'falls' into Switzerland. Violent and wonderful to behold. Through subterranean caves I went to get to a very insecure ledge almost underneath the hurtling waterfall to see it roar over the rocks.

"Then lunch in a famous fish restaurant where one could lean over from the table and caress the turquoise water. A pond from which to choose the handsomest blue trout and to sip while awaiting the chef's pleasure, a delicate white wine officially called St. Saphorn but more affectionately known as 'Charlie's Own', because it comes from the Swiss vineyard region where Chaplin lives. After indescribable joys of the melting trout yet another kind of fish is chosen from another pond and served in a soup-plate of butter – my poor waist is now quite unrecognisable – followed by wild strawberries and Chantilly cream, and a liqueur which just wrapped the whole meal up in silk . . ."

THE HAGUE

"I arrived in The Hague thinking to find the soft, quiet land of waterways and windmills and the soothing sway of many-coloured tulips under a cloudy sky, but never has Mrs. Preconception made a graver error. I find a gay, festive, scintillating town with more entertainment and nocturnal activity than I could ever have thought possible in the never-to-be-called-again Sober North.

"Ten minutes to glamour up and then into the Koninglijke Schouburg, once a ducal palace and now a royal theatre, to see the last performance by La Scala of Milan of Rossini's opera *L'Italiana in Algeri*.

"This was sparkling and full of the pizzicato brilliance of which the Italians are such masters, directed by Carlo Maria Giulini, who has not only the pulse of the music at his

122

finger-tips but also the heartstrings of every woman in the audience.

"Their reception – deservedly so – was fabulous. The public would not let them leave the stage and strewed it with flowers. The singers, in true Latin style, kissed them and threw them back to the audience amid screams of delight. I went back-stage to congratulate Giulini. It is rare to see the gods so kind to one individual, for they have bestowed on him youth, talent, grace, humour, and singular good looks.

"On to Scheveningen, which has more night-spots per head of population than almost anywhere. Dear Morpheus, forgive my sad neglect of you.

"This week I went into a tiny bar where a Hungarian sings and plays the piano in frenzied style with such speed that he uses not only his fingers but the backs of his hands and in extreme urgency his nose.

"And then to another, more dimly lit bar where I was initiated into the ecstasies of goldliquer (pronounced gold-digger.) This is a Dutch liqueur which has real gold leaf floating in it which you do not pick out and pay the bill but swallow down and dream of pinnacles and princes . . .

"To Delft and a fleeting and cursory glance at the 'Dream within a dream', looking exactly like a Vermeer interior in a frame of canals. The perfume of the limes was intoxicating . . . I was sad to say goodbye to The Hague and am *tout à fait d'accord* that it is the gayest and most wonderful 'village' in the world."

AMSTERDAM.

"In the midst of all this lies rather incongruously, a little flower-covered houseboat carefully tended by two elderly ladies living in it, with a large sign which reads: 'The Bible Club of Philadelphia'! The Dutch, of course, are highly efficient about these waterways which play so great a part in their lives. I was walking back from the theatre when I heard a loud cry. I turned just in time to see a woman back her car and plunge right into the canal. Two men dived in from a nearby flower barge and managed to extricate her, and within five minutes a sort of fire-engine-looking apparatus arrived and ladders, cranes and ropes brought a terrified and soaked woman and her car out of the water. This sort of thing happens twice a week, so no one was very concerned . . .

"On to Rotterdam and what moved me most was the soul-stirring statue by Ossip Zadkine which stands in the centre of the town. It symbolises 'Man's desperate struggle groping for the last refuge when earthly comforts have been destroyed'. It is the twisted, tortured body of a man with his heart and soul blown out of him; one hand implores and one hand protects. It stands about 40 ft high and has more strength than I have ever seen in modern sculpture . . ."

NORWAY.

"Our opening night of *Much Ado About Nothing* before the Crown Prince was followed by a soirée at Ambassador Sir Peter Scarlett's home – which was peopled with famous and romantic Norwegian names. Among them were Grieg, now chairman of the board of the theatre, a dear white-haired gentleman who has the same quality of personality as his ancestor had in music, and Mr. Alfred Maurstad, whom we nicknamed 'Papa Peer Gynt' because he plays the play with his own son playing himself as a young man in the first act. I saw this performance and it was just uncanny seeing these two men looking so alike playing virtually one man. It was very exciting.

"Ibsen, of course, is played a great deal and so the fact that Peggy Ashcroft braves the lion's den with an inspired interpretation of Hedda Gabler and was decorated for it by King Haakon makes her a kind of goddess, and she is spoken about in hushed, awed whispers.

"Probably the greatest exponent of Ibsen's female roles is his own grandson's wife, Lillebil Ibsen, with whom I had tea between the shows. I ventured to confess that the first time I set foot on a stage was in Ibsen at the age of six. I was delighted to hear she played the same part at nine years old. A woman of immense charm, with deep black hair and wide green eyes, very un-Nordic to look at, and who acts internationally in seven languages.

"The Norwegians are a people apart, born of a wild and savage country which cannot even feed her 3,000,000, and life is a continual struggle against the elements. They have a basic vitality and courage that breed men like Thor Heyerdahl, the Kon-Tiki king, and Knut Haugland, his wireless operator, who took me to see the unimaginable raft of strung-together balsa logs on which they lived for 101 days. To look at this unpretentious, thin, and unobtrusive man one would never envisage his extraordinary courage and it is only through the fire of his steel-blue eyes that I could see the spark which ignited the desire to venture across 4,000 miles of unchartered water to prove the migration of the Pacific. Only once did I see a sadness in their light, when he spoke of Heyerdahl's proposed expedition that he was unable to join. I asked him if, after his miraculous escape on the coral reef, he would knowingly, without the courage of ignorance, make a similar expedition and he said: 'Oh yes, a hundred times.'

"But of all the Norwegians I have met the most fascinating, and yet, perhaps, the most typical, has been Jan Daalsrud, the hero of *We Die Alone*, the greatest epic of escape and endurance of the war.

"This fabulous war hero sat here in my dressing room at the theatre and debunked his whole story, as though it had been as easy as falling off the proverbial log, until I found myself asking him quite lightly why during his escape through the snows he had cut off only nine of his ten gangrenous toes with his penknife. He replied he wanted to hang on to the tenth as a souvenir. Now he has a film as a souvenir, because British Lion bought the film rights and have immortalised the story of this

24-year-old Norwegian boy who, as a result of working in the Resistance, suffered such unbelievable privations. I asked him why particularly he had volunteered for this work. He explained that if one knuckles down under Occupation one is apt to lose one's soul.

"So, with these fighting words from a fighting spirit, I write my last words on a European tour and I fly happily back into my own little family shell."

Getting to know Sir John Gielgud was a time that I treasure. He had a great wry sense of humour, loved puns and punning. One day while I was writing away at my article, he watched me awhile then said, "Careful, dear girl, you'll get Reuter's cramp!" He was an avid doer of *The Times* crossword. He used to come off after the first act of *King Lear* with tears streaming down his face, and without even wiping them away would make straight for the crossword and fill in a word.

One night when we were going to make an excursion to the Bertold Brecht Theatre in East Berlin, we nearly lost Sir John altogether. The only way to get there was by tube, and we were given strict instructions not to take the train marked Potsdam because we would be held by the Russians and it would maybe take weeks to extricate us. We walked into the station and a train came in which was very clearly labelled "Potsdam". Sir John, as if making a final exit from the cruel world around him, stepped grandly on to the train, and the doors closed behind him. We all looked on horrified, and when his face turned back to us through the window in terror we knew that he hadn't realised what he had done. But it was too late, the train was already gone. All his banging on the window was to no avail. We were all distraught as we had to give a performance the next day to say nothing of all the tortures we imagined he was going to have to suffer at the hands of the Russians. Miserably we all got on the right train and at the next station there was standing a very white and shaken Sir

John! He had caught the only *stopping* train to Potsdam of the month!

It was during this season that I had the first warning signs that my nerves were in danger. I started to be afraid to go on the stage, afraid I would forget my lines and even when I was on the stage I was unable to listen to what the other actors were saying because all the time I would have to keep repeating the line I was to say next over and over again. I hid this from everyone, hoping it didn't show too much. George Devine, a wonderful and understanding man – what a void his death left in the theatre and to his friends – noticed and tried to help me. But the balance of nerves is such a delicate thing. Without them artists aren't any good and with too much of them they can be destroyed. I was getting to destruction point. Looking back on it now it was probably the result of going back to work too soon after having a baby. However, when the season ended, I started turning down work. I was asked to play Joan of Arc, but I refused because I knew I would never get through it. I turned down several other roles as well. I had decided to become a cabbage and give up altogether. Until one day a friend suggested I go to see a hypnotist. I scoffed, but he insisted on making an appointment. "Don't be put off by the hypnotist's appearance," he warned. I arrived in Harley Street to find a great big hearty Irishman of about eighty – standing on one leg! Before we started the session he showed me pictures of himself on the wall in the boxing ring, before and after his leg had been amputated! His passion had been amateur boxing and he was taken prisoner in the First World War after having lost his leg. He was so determined to get back that he studied hypnotism while a prisoner of war, and when he came out, he had overcome his physical disability to such an extent that he went back in the ring and became known as the one-legged boxer! Well that was almost enough for me. I hardly needed the session after that. I thought, if he can get over a physical disability to such an extent, I, with all my arms and legs, can certainly get over a nervous one. I just need my mind straightening out! I felt better already. He put me in a semi-trance and simply by talking to me removed the fears that were lurking in my brain. After six visits, I was ready to play the unabridged version of *War and Peace*.

The next job that came up I grabbed. It was doing a TV Spectacular with Bob Hope and Maurice Chevalier! What a pair! Bob had sixteen men with him wherever he went. They all moved as one man, three gag writers among them with the most strained expressions I've ever seen on three men's faces. They were paid to be and find funnies. So they felt bound every time they opened their mouths to say something hilarious. The pressure was killing them. Bob knew this and teased them relentlessly. But Bob told me an enchanting story about his youngest daughter aged seven, having watched him finish a golf tournament, as he walked off the course she greeted him with, "Hello, Bob Hope," which of course got a big laugh. Bob took her aside and told her she must call him Daddy and not Bob Hope in front of people. Crestfallen the little girl said, "O.K., Daddy. I know, you gotta get all the laughs."

He is a great man and a laugh a line on and off stage. Kind and generous, he bought me a gorgeous bottle of perfume after the show. We went to Paris to rehearse with Maurice. Dear Maurice kindly invited us to lunch, and Bob said, "Mind if I bring the boys?" Maurice rather apprehensively said, "How many does that make us for lunch?" Bob said, "Just eighteen!"

When the press came to take pictures, Bob took me in his arms and said, "Shall I kiss you now or shall I tease you a little first!"

I reminded Maurice of the first time we met. It was at a party after *The Colonels*. It was late at night, I was tired, there were a lot of people and the apartment was rather dark. I was sitting very squashed on a settee, talking to the man on my right, when I felt a knee rubbing my knee on my left. I didn't take any notice, until it happened again. Then I thought, some dreary man trying to make a pass, so I ignored it again, until the third time I determined to give him a piece of my mind. I swung round and did the biggest double take in the world. It was Chevalier himself who was indulging in the latin sport of kneesy, kneesy! I was delighted; my knees had never caught me such a big fish – before or since!! We have been great chums ever since!

Chapter 14

My life has a strange habit of repeating itself. Things seem to happen in pairs. The first was that my own mother was engaged to a French Marquis who lived about thirty kilometres from where my Vicomte lived. She ran away from hers, I ran away from mine the first time I met him. She regretted not having married hers, I don't regret having married mine. Second, quite unconsciously (of the date that is, not my state of health) I got married on the same date as my mother – December 23rd. Jacques and I broke down in our car in a blinding snowstorm near Grenoble, and three years later broke down at precisely the same spot, in a rainstorm. And now I had just taken on a new play at the Criterion called *Paddle Your Own Canoe*. It had been open exactly one month, I had the same dressing room and almost to the day, I fell pregnant again. But this time I did actually lose it, to my great and deep sorrow. So in order to get over the depression which was unbearable I decided to launch my own one-woman show and tour the world. The idea started with a series of classic stories I adapted for television. And I had shared a theatre programme at an Ingestre Festival with a singer – I did three stories and she did the equivalent time in songs. At that festival was a European impresario who invited me to go to The Hague for the British Festival and to do the whole programme alone. I told her she was out of her mind, that I couldn't hold a stage alone for two and a quarter hours. She persuaded me I could, so, once the challenge was accepted, I got cracking. I chose seven well-balanced stories of different authors and mood. A de Maupassant, an Edgar Allan Poe, d'Almeida, Dorothy Parker, etc. In each one the basic theme was love, whether it was love of money, or a man, or the bottle, or a horse, it didn't matter. I called the programme *People in Love*. I designed portable sets, chose music to accompany the stories, designed a wardrobe with a change for each character, bought twelve spotlights, sound equipment and amplifiers. And put the whole thing together preparatory to going to The Hague. Then I started to worry about never having tried out the whole programme before opening at the Festival. A streak of light descended on me and I telephoned the Governor of Holloway Jail! Here I was assured of a truly captive audience who would be forced to hear me out to the end! She was delighted and the following Sunday afternoon, I had my gala première in the precincts of the jail. The show has never gone so well. They adored it, laughed and cried in all the right places and gave me all the courage to go forward and attack the world!

I think the psychological effect of seeing all those poor women locked up gave me an added spirit, making me realise how lucky I was. There must have been five hundred of them, all neatly dressed in the blue uniform. Above their heads between the floors of cells was strung a sort of chicken netting. This apparently was to deter them committing suicide by jumping over. I looked into one of the cells before the show and saw a girl with curlers in her hair, putting nail varnish on her nails. I thought, well that's not so bad, until I looked on her door which simply gave her number, and underneath it was written "five years". I realised then how much she needed those curlers and that varnish. Part of the old Victorian horror they had attempted to brighten up by painting the walls in sort of Neapolitan colours. I was not shown the bad parts where the unruly cases were but I heard the screams. It was very disturbing. The first offenders' block was marvellous. No bars, open door and windows and proper beds, two to a room with lovely cards on the mantlepiece saying, "Come home soon,

Mum." Here they played cards or scrabble or made things. The Governor, far from being a stern harridan as one would imagine, seemed a very gentle creature who was all out to help the women. She had a daughter called Melba. I asked her why she had chosen that name and it appeared that as a young man her husband had heard Melba sing and had fallen in love with her, and vowed that if ever he had a daughter he would call her Melba. So even in Holloway Jail the theatre has left its little mark.

The opening in Holland was marvellous for me because it was a very sophisticated audience and yet the programme seemed to please them as much. The notices were fabulous and my star was sailing high. I did a few weeks in the provinces in England to play it in, then booked twelve weeks in South Africa. In fact, it did so well that I did fourteen months in South Africa and Australia and covered seventy five thousand miles, mostly by car. Little Chantal and Nanny and Jacques came to join us, and had a glorious time.

In South Africa I had a huge station wagon on which we loaded absolutely everything. My stage manager and assistant and myself sat in the front, and all we needed was a bare stage and electricity and we were away. My advance bookings and publicity were done by that little ball of fire Anna Romain Hoffman, and we played every day, mostly travelling by day three to five hundred miles, arriving at four p.m., setting up the show, doing an evening performance, then while I attended the mayoral reception the boys would repack and we would drive off to the next town. Of course in the big cities we stayed several weeks, but I specially wanted to take theatre to people who had never seen a live performance. And indeed they drove eighty and a hundred miles just to see the show. One night in Zululand I was doing a performance for the natives and everything was going well until I got to the Edgar Allan Poe story which is about a man who buries the heart of his master under the floorboards. The heart-beat gets louder and louder until he goes mad. Well, I put the heart-beat on record and while I tell the story the momentum of the beat increases until it reaches breaking point. To my horror I suddenly realised that all the natives were joining in every time the heart beat and they were getting more and more excited and were now rising in their seats and getting louder and louder. And by the time it came to its climax they had broken into a full Zulu war dance. I ran off the stage and got the organisers to calm them down before I was thrown into the boiling pot!

On our way up to play the Rhodesias we were driving on the strip roads (they can't afford to make entire roads, so only two strips the size of car tyres are macadamised) doing eighty miles an hour when we had a tyre burst. The car turned over on its side and hung dangerously over the side of a pretty steep precipice. I was crying somewhat hysterically from shock and relief. The boys dragged me out of the car and put me on a rug by the side of the road, while they tried to right the car. Just then another car came along with two men and a woman. The men helped with the car and the woman came to help me. She gave me some tea from her Thermos and all I could keep saying was, "The theatre, we must get to the theatre." The woman stopped in her tracks, turned to me and said, "You're not Moira Lister, are you?" "Yes," I said weakly. "Oh, how marvellous – *lie* where you are while I go and get my camera!"

Then an extraordinary thing happened at Victoria Falls. We made the theatre in time and at the reception afterwards the Mayor asked us if his son-in-law could take some pictures of me at the "Falls" for the local paper. I agreed on condition that we do it at eight-thirty a.m. as we were leaving. The photographer agreed readily, saying he had another appointment at nine a.m. He collected me in his car. He had a cold, and seemed rather depressed and uncommunicative. However, he took the pictures and promised to send me copies and off I went. A week later a copy of the local paper was sent to me with my picture in it at the Falls, and on another page the report that the photographer who had taken it had in fact committed suicide at nine a.m. on that same morning by jumping over the Falls! That was his appointment!

The other suicide on the tour was equally bizarre. It was at the Kimberley Big Hole, which is the place where the original diamonds were found. The bottom of the hole has water in it. It is I think something like a mile deep before you get to the water. And the tourist attraction is to throw a huge boulder down and watch it become a pebble before it hits the water. Well, this day we were doing just that when I noticed what looked like two crossed matchsticks on top of the water. I looked through the binoculars and my stomach turned when I discovered it was the body of a man lying splayed out on top of the water. I asked the guide and he confirmed that a man had committed suicide a fortnight before and that they couldn't get him out even with a helicopter as the suction was too great so they just had to wait until the body disintegrated and so sink to the bottom. Ugh!

My entrance into Ladysmith caused quite a stir. Completely unintentional, it looked like the publicity gimmick of the year! We had been driving most of the night and all day and I was beginning to get claustrophobia about being inside the car. I had to get out. As we were about – I thought – three miles outside of Ladysmith I told the boys to drop me, go on ahead, set up, and I would *walk* in. Reluctantly they did – pointing out the dangers of a woman alone on an open road. I pooh-poohed it all and insisted they leave me. The first mile went very well, although every time a native passed on a bicycle or car I waved to a cow on the horizon pretending my dearest friends were next to it. I also turned my ring on the inside as I realised it flashed rather brightly in the sun as I waved and didn't want to be murdered just for an old diamond! Well, the second and third miles passed and now the blisters on my feet were beginning to assume bulbous proportions. I took my shoes off.

The burning road made it worse. I walked on – I had obviously mistaken the mileage – until I literally couldn't walk another step. I sat down knowing I wasn't going to make the show. Then over the horizon came an enormous horse with a native boy riding it. That is the answer! I waited until they got to me and then tried to persuade the rider to lend me the horse. He was not interested; he had just ridden five miles out of Ladysmith and didn't want to go all the way back. Finally I promised to give him five pounds when we got to Ladysmith; even this he was dubious about. And it was only when I took off my earrings and gave them to him to wear that I got a big smile, and the horse. So I rode astride this huge grey mare right up to the town hall where the Mayor and congregation were on the steps to greet me. And as I arrived I was showered with applause! Very original entrance, they all congratulated me. I didn't have the heart to show them my blisters!

While I was playing the Eastern Transvaal we all went to the Game Reserve. This is a unique experience in itself, but I had a uniquer one! One lives in thatched huts in a camp inside the Reserve where the wild animals roam at liberty. At night you sit round the open fire and cook your meal. This is called a Braaivleis. You go to sleep to the accompaniment of jungle noises and wake up in the morning about five ready to go off in the car to see the animals – with strict instructions to keep inside your car and not open windows. Well, we'd had a marvellous morning seeing lion, giraffe, elephant, masses of springbok and just as we were returning there was a lazy hyena sitting high on a bank just next to my window. It was a fabulous picture. Four-year-old Chantal was sitting on my lap, and I stupidly rolled down the window to get a good camera angle. As I clicked the camera the hyena snarled, I got a fright and rolled the window up hurriedly but in my panic caught Chantal's head right on the window. She screamed. That frightened the hyena and he made one leap for her face. By the grace of God I managed to release her head and roll the window up just as his claws lashed down the window pane. What a horrible moment. I have often thought about it since, how devastating it would have been if she had had her face disfigured and I would have had to answer the question for the rest of my life, "What happened to your child's face?". And I would have had to say, "Eaten by an hyena."

What an incredible experience this tour of South Africa was. I played every available town – the gold-fields where they told me if I could pick up a gold brick with one hand it was mine. I tried desperately hard so to do, but had no luck. Whenever we played near a big mine the managers would arrange a Zulu war dance for us by the mine boys who took great pride in performing. It was marvellous to watch under those circumstances but I wouldn't like to be among them on a dark night! Not after my experience in Zululand. We went to ostrich farms and I actually rode on the back of an ostrich. It reminded me of when I was a little girl and my father's great game was to put me on the back of one and go into gales of laughter as the ostrich ran away with me clinging to its neck. We ate omelettes made of ostrich eggs which are the equivalent in size of twelve hens eggs. Playing in the Transkei, which is now the Bantutian state, we went into a real witch-doctor's shop, and I had never seen such a collection of weird objects in my life – dried bones, hens' feet, frog's legs, herbs of every sort. While I was there a native woman came in with her new-born baby still in the bloodstained swaddling clothes. The woman paid two and sixpence and was given a handful of what looked like crystallised soil. I asked our interpreter what it was. He hedged, saying he wouldn't like to tell me, but explained that it was something the native women ate for six weeks before the birth and six weeks after, and this entirely stopped all labour pain. Now I really had to know and was all prepared to patent it for my European sisters to help them with their pangs. But when he told me I rather went off the idea. It was actually baboon's urine that was collected from the caves and apparently had the necessary chemical requirements. Another morsel of information he gave me was that if a mother dies in childbirth he had another herb which he gave to the grandmother and she would start to lactate and so be able to feed the child. I didn't think any of my grandmother friends in Europe would be mad about the idea either, so I didn't pursue it.

The Transkei is the red blanket country where all the natives wear these beautiful deep coral blankets which are dyed with the flowers of the aloes; the original idea was so that other tribes would not be able to distinguish them from the tall red spike of the aloe. The young girls are taught to open the tops of these blankets and show their bare breasts. If the breasts are not quite up to standard they only ask sixpence, but you can gaze on a pretty fulsome pair for one and six!

We went through the citrus areas where in one game reserve a herd of wild elephants comes through the scrub every night at six o'clock for a feast of oranges. These are delivered in lorries, then fed through a large pipe from the warden's house to the other side of the high wire fencing, and the elephants have a great game picking them up in their trunks and popping them into their mouths. From there I went up into the Rhodesias. This was just before Zambia was formed. In Southern Rhodesia I stayed with the Courtaulds in Umtali and played the beautiful little theatre they have given to the country together with a superb art gallery. Some of the smaller towns were fascinating. One I particularly remember because it had a little chapel which had been decorated by local natives and all the murals were of Jesus and Mary and the apostles, and they were all black! After Salisbury I went on into Northern Rhodesia, now Zambia, and played a large town hall in Bulawayo, then into the Copper Belt which is an extraordinary territory where the ant hills which still contain live and active ants are larger than the three to four bedroom bungalows that are built cheek by jowl to them. I went down a copper mine which I hated. I was terrified. I can't stand a lot of giant-size machinery. Then I popped over the border into the Congo and played one of the most beautiful theatres I've ever seen, in Elisabethville. Designed by a Belgian architect it was a unique idea for a six-hundred seater, which by using the same stage and simply raising the back wall and reversing the stage became an outdoor theatre for two thousand people. I was the first person to play there in English. I dread to think what it is used for now. In Ndola we were taken for a sail on one of their lakes but told to be very careful not to put hands or feet in the water as it was thick with crocodiles – in fact, I got some marvellous cine pictures of the crocodiles from the boat.

Having done my first round trip I then went back on it all over again to make a series of half-hour films for the B.B.C. called *Theatre on Safari*. These I made. The B.B.C. paid their option and then unfortunately Sharpeville happened and nobody would touch anything to do with South Africa. So I still have them as a fabulous memento of a fabulous tour.

It was while I was in South Africa that a theatrical impresario invited me to continue my tour and do all the capital cities in Australia. I was thrilled with the idea as I had never been to Australia and also it would be a chance to visit my sister Evelyn who lives in Tasmania. So I readily accepted. Jacques, Chantal and Nanny decided it was best for them to take a house by the sea in Hout Bay in South Africa while I did the Australian tour and if it went well to come and join me. So we shipped everything off and the boys and I took the plane to Perth. En route we spent a day in the beautiful volcanic island of Mauritius. We drove through miles of sugar-cane fields with big mounds of black lava among them. We visited Government House and picked mangoes with a long pole with a little basket at the end, and then rode on the back of the two-hundred-and-fifty-year-old tortoise. It is a real lush tropical island, pale blue lagoons and swaying palm trees and filled with local colour; Indians, Chinese, French all bringing something of their culture to the buildings, food and markets. I bought two superb Indian saris. And so on to Cocos Island which is simply a landing strip in the middle of the ocean, and then Perth. Here the whole aspect of my tour changed. It was now big business. I was met by a man who was to be my own press representative at £100 a week to handle my show exclusively. He had organised the press who were there "en force" to interview me. I only stayed the day and went on to Sydney where I was to open. He travelled with me and handed me an itinerary which took my breath away. Apart from all the press, television and radio interviews, he had also got me a desk in the leading newspaper office in every city as he had secured a daily article for me to write throughout the country. On any subject I liked: food, clothes, wines, theatre, children, Zulus, animals, psychiatry – that he left up to me! Also he had leapt on the idea that my husband was in champagne, and every town I hit he arranged for the press to photograph me having champagne and angel cake for breakfast! This was no hardship! All the women's clubs invited me to talk to them. This meant an hour's talk practically every morning, as well as the in-vitations from so many kind people. But how it paid off! The theatres were crammed and I was playing vast auditoriums and we did wonderful business.

Of course there were the usual amusing incidents that are part and parcel of theatre life. I was asked to do a television show in Sydney. The producer met me with great enthusiasm saying, "Oh, Moira, how wonderful it is to have you here – please forgive me calling you Moira, but I just feel I know you so well. You're so clever, so versatile. You have your one-woman show, and all the films you've done. Marvellous. Now before we go into the studio do sign your autograph for me." I took his book and was just about to sign it when he said, "Tell me, when are you going to do Giselle!" I couldn't bear to disappoint him so I signed his book Moira Shearer and gave it back to him. When we got into the studio there was an audience of five hundred and with great pride he walked up to the mike and introduced me as Moira Shearer. Well, again I didn't want to make him look a fool in front of all those people, so I let it go and simply did the show as Moira Shearer. After the performance an old lady came up to me, took my hand and said, "Miss Shearer, what an honour to have you in our country. I have admired you for so long, but of all the things you have ever done the one I remember best was your superb performance in *Smiling Through*" (Norma Shearer!!).

I was at last able to test the old adjunct that oysters are an aphrodisiac. I literally lived on them in Sydney because they come out of the harbour there and are delicious and very cheap. But I must be quite honest. I did not find myself climbing the walls or sending cables to get my husband over. All I did was to collect some super recipes of how to do them in a hundred different ways. The oysters I mean!

I got across to Tasmania for the weekend and saw my sister and her four boys. What fabulous-looking chaps! Says a lot for the kind of outdoor life they lead, sailing, swimming, golfing. And what a lovely island, almost reminiscent of parts of Devon. It was all too short before I had to get back to the grind. But the grind was not too painful in this great continent. There was so much to see and do apart from the theatre. Sydney with its staggering harbour and the beautiful modern homes built all round it. Not good for swimming – too many sharks – but very picturesque. Some amazing art collections and my introduction to Nolan, the strange Australian painter of haunting talent. The women all very chic with the latest imports from Paris and Rome and all the money with which to buy them. A weekend on a sheep station. I didn't know sheep could be cooked in so many different ways. Out on the outback a feeling of tremendous peace. A vast nothingness where you alone seem to exist – it's an odd feeling and I can understand its attraction and danger for people who live there. Brisbane with its houses built on stilts to create some air in an over humid climate. Possums coming out from the bush to eat at your table.

Surfer's Paradise, a cacophony of vibrant colour. Every house seems to have an original mixture of paints. A superb beach and bright glaring modern establishments around it. Melbourne more stately and reminiscent of England. And the few remaining buildings which are shown with pride now as antiques because they were "convict" built. A tremendous cosmopolitan population who are referred to as new Australians and not altogether popular with perhaps the more indolent old Australians, because they work harder and earn more money. Of course I was given presents of boomerangs, rather grand ones, engraved, and a whole school of Koala bears. The children adored them. But in all a country of the future where almost anyone with the will to work and something to offer can thrive and thrive well.

After four terribly strenuous months there, I had another breakdown of nerves. This was much more severe than the first. I was on stage at the first house on Saturday, and had got to the end of the first act, just to the climax of the Edgar Allan Poe story where in fact the character goes mad, when suddenly I went completely paralysed. I couldn't move, my whole body was stiff. I couldn't speak or move my jaw. I just stood there completely immobile. Ironically the audience thought it was part of the mad scene and applauded wildly, as the boys (who realised something was wrong) brought the curtain down. They rushed on to the stage and carried me to my dressing room. They gave me brandy and gradually my body came out of its rigid state into a state of collapse and with it I started to cry and couldn't stop. I had the ignominy of having to send a bewildered audience home after the first half. They were offered their money back. We cancelled the evening show and I was carried home where doctors and osteopaths were brought in to try to get me back on my feet. I was given injections and massage and fortifiers, calmers and stimulants, until by the time Monday came I insisted on going back to the theatre. From then on my performance became a terror for me as I kept waiting for the paralysis to happen again. I would go out on stage and see a vast sea of faces and say, "Please God let me get through," and between each story I said a Hail Mary as I changed my clothes. Fortunately the tour had only a few more days to go, and in fact because of my fears the intensity of my acting was heightened so I was in fact giving better performances towards the end. I got so depressed that I convinced myself I had a tumour on the brain and wouldn't be alive to see my husband and child again. However, it all ended without further incident, with a big send-off from Perth, and a sell-out fortnight there. So that when I actually got on the plane to go home I regretted not having accepted the New Zealand and country tour of Australia. I would love to go back and do that one day. But after fourteen months of twenty thousand words memorised per night plus matinées plus promotion plus travelling seventy-five thousand miles, I really was too tired to do anything but lie in the sun on a beach in South Africa with the security of my family and regain my strength.

Chapter 15

I T took longer than I anticipated to get back to normal. In fact I readily spent three months as the guest of Hazel Vyvian in her lovely house in Kloof, Natal, which is near the Valley of a Thousand Hills. A warm, humid climate and immaculately styled native servants to answer every call. A pool in the garden and the sea within close proximity. Gradually my nerves regained their resilience, although through a lot of soul-searching I decided it was time to give up my career while at the height and settle down and have two more children which I dearly wanted and Chantal needed. I had reconciled myself to this and when I felt strong again we left for London via Paris. While in Paris, however, all resolutions went overboard. It didn't take much! One night in Paris I went to the theatre alone to see *Becket*. I was given a box to myself. I sat up there so enthralled by what I saw that I found myself saying, "What am I doing up here, I am on the wrong side of the curtain. I should be there on that stage, that's where I belong." So naturally when I got back to London and I was asked to meet Ian Carmichael with a view to starring opposite him in the American comedy *The Gazebo*, I readily accepted. Ian came to the flat and from the moment he walked in a kind of electricity sparked. We had the same sense of humour, the same attitude and knowledge of comedy. He came with the producer Anthony Sharp for a quick drink and ostensibly to look me over! They stayed for three hours, and when they left Ian and Tony were convinced that I was the right leading lady.

So away we went into *The Gazebo* under the management of that human dynamo, Harold Fielding, who I think is one of the greatest impresarios of our day. To me he is one of the few men in England who has the courage to launch the show in which he believes. He believes in spending money to make money. He gets to the heart of the public by unashamed publicity. We have this strange obsession in England that anything good should be kept a dead secret. Like the best Savile Row tailor would never dream of advertising, the best clubs like Whites, Boodles, Pratts, go on the principle that people in the know, know, and the rest don't exist, but this doesn't work for the theatre. The public's imagination must be captured by how a show is presented. A great example of this is the recent launching of Ginger Rogers playing *Mame*. Fielding has so whetted the appetite of the public to go and sample this show that in fact he has made it critic proof. And I write this *before* it opens. So that my predictions of its success can be measured. And he did the same for us with *The Gazebo*. Not to the same extent – it wasn't necessary as it was a slight comedy thriller – but proportionately the story was the same. We ran for fourteen months and could have run much longer if Ian hadn't decided, quite naturally, he wanted to do something fresh. But in fact, from a purely selfish point of view, the fact that his place was taken by Alan Melville was a great stroke of luck for me because it was from those days of fun and understanding of me by Alan that the seeds of our Very Merry Widow came. But that was seven years before. So to stay with *The Gazebo* for a moment. Ian has probably been the one leading man with whom I have had complete theatrical rapport. Now this may sound lightly said but it is an almost impossible wavelength to define. Comedy is the most difficult medium to play. So when one finds someone who works the same way, one clings to it with great tenacity. The understanding of feeding a comedy line, then getting the laugh, then milking it, then stopping the audience laughing so as to build to the next comedy line, is an almost intangible thing. Inexplicable and un- teachable. It is there or not there. And we had it for each other,

Moments I treasure most

Ian Carmichael. He's Gem
I'm a Leo – need I say mo

Derek Nimmo. He's a Vir
you'd never know it!

so that our work on the stage was enormously exciting and satisfying. We have since done five shows together and always they have proved a complete experience.

Whether the public has always liked them is another matter. But whether they've been successful or not we've had the satisfaction of giving our best and interpreting our authors to the best of our joint abilities.

The Savoy Theatre is wonderful to play. Everyone naturally imagines we dine in the Grill every night; this is not absolutely true, although on the occasions I have, I always found something amusing to report the next day. For instance – one night a frightfully dashing fellah came up to me and said, "I say, I've just seen your piece and dashed amusing it was. Now this chap Carmichael, I've seen him around quite a lot, films, television, stage. I say, does he enjoy actin'?" "Well, yes," I said. "I think so." "Well, I do hope so, because it does seem to take up an awful lot of his time!"

I had been in the play about six months when I discovered I was going to have another baby.

Naturally I was very thrilled by the news but apprehensive of losing it again, so I determined not to say anything to a single soul so that I would have no emotional disturbance. I tried to lead a very healthy life. Rested till the theatre at night, walked to and from the theatre each day to get my muscles firm, gave up smoking and drinking. And my darling old dresser, whom I'd had for sixteen years, was the only one who knew my secret. She and I would knit "tiny garments" which were hurriedly hidden when anyone came in. I went around with a seraphic smile on my face and it became a kind of game with me as to how long I could go without anyone finding out. But my game only lasted five months and once more I was bereft of what I wanted most in the world. Another child. I was taken off to a nursing home and all hope of keeping it was clinically removed. I came home after three days and while appreciating the wonderful flowers that surrounded my bed and the kind attention of my husband, I became suffocated by them, and felt I was in a morgue. I had to get out. So one day when no one was about I packed my bags, took a taxi and with tears streaming down my face bought a ticket to Nice and cried all the way there, got into another taxi and said, still crying, "Drive me to the nearest beach." He looked surprised and said the first sandy beach was Juan-les-Pins. "That will do," I said. And so I arrived in Juan. Walked into the first hotel, threw down my bag, checked in and went straight to the beach where I virtually lay for ten days. The sun has always been a great healer for me and gradually I came out of my torpor and realised I had to get on with life, and how lucky I was to have one beautiful child already, and a kind and wonderful husband, and so many other blessings, that I took a great pull on myself and went back to London and to work.

After a year in *The Gazebo*, Alan Melville took over Ian's role. I was pretty chary of meeting him, after all his successes in the field of rapier wit and satirical humour. But in fact I need never have worried. He moved in and within a week it felt like he'd always been there. We had fun. He had a marvellous man-servant who used to make fantastic food for us between shows on matinée days. So this became a kind of ritual. People used to drop in at that time and it was like a miniature Sardis, where the dialogue was as good as the dishes. He lived in Brighton and every night I used to drive him to Victoria from the Savoy in seven minutes flat. Of course red lights were discounted and any late zebra-crossers had their pants smartly shined but otherwise we always arrived without incident, or not any that I noticed anyway.

So *The Gazebo* came to an end. During all the theatre runs, of course, were the television plays which were rehearsed during the day and transmitted on Sundays. During this period I made *The Apple Cart* with darling Jack Hawkins playing Magnus, and how good he was too. The strength that he brought to the role is the same innate fortitude with which he has so successfully overcome his operation and has been able to pick up his career again. Who says actors aren't a strong breed of men!

Now came another stage play called *Critic's Choice*. And this time we'd only got into the first two weeks of rehearsal when my hopes were confirmed and I was again in an interesting condition! But now my doctor was extremely firm. "If you want this child you go to bed and stay there for six months," was his verdict. So torn between the two choices I didn't really hesitate very long and took to my bed. And happily it paid off and at the end I was able to hold in my arms my second little seven-pound bundle whom we called Christobel. The actual night of the birth, looking back on it now, was quite amusing because this time I was determined not to go through that long waiting period in the nursing home so decided to stay at home as long as possible. In fact the first stages of labour started on the Friday night, but they were very slight so I didn't take much notice. All the next day at regular intervals I had twinges. I rang my doctor and told him I would come as soon as they got bad. So Saturday evening I was watching the last programme on television which was a superb production of Somerset Maugham's *The Moon and Sixpence* when I went into the second stages of labour. But I was so enjoying the play I just dug my nails into the chair every ten minutes and insisted on seeing the finish. The play ended around midnight, and I stood up and said "Right! Quick! The nursing home!" By now the pains were coming thick and fast. Of course to find a taxi at midnight on a Saturday was not easy. Jacques was running round the Square – so was my Spanish nanny. By this time I was on the floor. However, just in time Jacques found one and bundled me in and said to the driver, "Go very slowly." Obviously trying to ease my pain. I came out of my rigor long enough to yell, "Slowly? You fool! For Christ's sake give it all the speed you've got." We made it, and arrived just in time for her to pop out on to a lovely starched bed – beautifully and naturally.

Now my cup was full, indeed brimming over. I was so fulfilled I felt I could climb the highest mountain. But not being quite so sportive, four weeks after she was born I was starring opposite Nigel Patrick in *Zero Hour* instead. In fact I was so full of the joys of spring that I wanted to do something very energetic. So I accepted a revue devised by Charles Ross called *See you Inside*. We went out on tour with it for six weeks and I had a ball. I danced, sang, did point numbers and thoroughly camped up the whole thing. I really enjoyed every minute of it. We had a great and talented cast with Amanda Barrie, Jon Pertwee, Mary Miller, Harold Lang, John Dane and myself. Unfortunately there was no theatre available at the time we wanted to come in, so the show closed with the idea of getting it together again when a theatre became vacant. But in the meantime I was asked to do *Devil May Care* with Ian Carmichael by Alan Melville at the Strand. This was one of those plays that was a near miss. It was almost right but not quite. However, we squeezed a few months out of it and then it folded.

As a little indication of how much on the same wavelength Ian and I were while working, on the opening night of *Devil May Care* it is the custom to give the other artists a little token good-luck present. Now I live almost next to Harrods. Ian lives in Mill Hill and very rarely comes to town. I went into Harrods, walked all over the store and eventually tucked away in the glass department I found what I thought would be appropriate. It was a white opaque beaker, with the music of Faustus printed on it. I thought this would be fun as he was playing the Devil. There were two of them side by side on the shelf. I bought one, had it wrapped and sent it to Ian's dressing room for the opening night. When I arrived in my dressing room amid flowers and presents and telegrams, I found Ian's present. I opened it and it was the *other* identical white opaque beaker. He had gone to Harrods, walked all over the store and ended up in the same tucked-away corner in the glass department about an hour after me! Strange!

Now I was feeling the urge to go home again to South Africa mainly because I wanted to show Daddy his new grandchild, and I had been offered a play there written by Muriel and Sydney Box called *Bedtime Story* – a two-hander for man and woman. I was doing a film at the time called *Joey Boy*, and in it was a young actor who I always thought very good. He was ideal casting for the part. His name was Derek Nimmo. I asked him if he was interested in going to South Africa. He seemed very keen, and having read the play accepted. We rehearsed in London and to my great joy I found my intuition was right and that he had the same sense of comedy as Ian. And so I rather took it on myself to encourage the director Hugh Goldie to let him do slightly outrageous things in the play and let himself go much further than he had ever done before and by this I don't mean he was taking his trousers down, I simply mean he was broadening his comedy to embellish the role. One day while rehearsing he had to remove his shoes and socks and I looked at those great long toes of his and said, "My God, you're deformed. See if you can do anything with them, for instance at this moment in the play if you could do 'Here's the church, here's the steeple, here's the preacher, and here are the people' WITH YOUR TOES – it would be fabulous." He tried and the result was hilarious. He has used his toes many times since; they even stole an Eamonn Andrews show from Bob Hope and Bing Crosby. We got to South Africa and did the play there and Derek was an instant success. They loved him and all the comedy business that we had all put in worked very well. One night I was waiting to go on and Derek, who entered two minutes after me, was not there. I heard a great commotion going on downstairs and found Derek in a state of agitation because the dresser had washed his socks and under-pants, and they were still wringing wet. "I can't go on," he said. I got very angry, and said, "Get on and don't make such a fuss – so if you haven't got any underpants on who cares." "I can't go on stage in a pair of pyjamas with no underpants." "All right," I yelled. "Wear a pair of mine." I dashed into my dressing room and all I could find was a pair of very lacy briefs. He put these on and made his entrance. Everything went well until we got to the pyjama scene. And although he never removed his pyjamas I kept getting this mental picture of what he must have looked like underneath in my frilly pants. Needless to say I could hardly get through the scene.

One night in Cape Town a cricket joined in the act. It was under the stage, and every time Derek or I would pause this damn cricket would chirp loud and clear. It was ridiculous. So much so that the audience started to enjoy the joke and every time it chirped they went into gales of laughter, so of course did we on stage. During the interval twenty men went under the stage to try to kill it. But it was too smart. It only performed with the curtain up. It was a hysterical evening.

On the last night in Cape Town after the show we'd had a party back-stage and we were all in pretty high spirits so I challenged Derek to a race home, which was thirteen miles of the most precipitous cliff all along the sea from Cape Town to Hout Bay to the beautiful home of Joyce Muller where we were staying. There are no lights on the road and it is highly dangerous. But we'd had a marvellous and successful tour and I was feeling a bit light-headed as it was the last night. I had a Ford, which a kind gentleman whom I'd sat next to in the plane from Johannesburg to Cape Town had lent me for my stay, and Derek had hired a mini. Of course it was sheer madness but off we went and just as we were nearing Hout Bay, having gone the whole way at maximum speed round the bends trying to pass each other, and driving parallel and in short behaving like maniacs – how we weren't both killed I shall never know – we suddenly heard a police siren behind us. Naturally we both pulled up expecting the worst. Two police officers ran to my car and without a word to me threw open all the doors and the boot, then ran to Derek's car and did the same. Derek and I waited dumbfounded. They came back, apologised, said they were looking for two prostitutes, and they thought we had given them a lift. Just at that moment Jacques arrived in a very Latin fury to chastise us for behaving like idiots. His hands, expressive at the gentlest of times, went up into the air, his vocabulary, which you would have had to be a French scholar to understand even at dictation speed, became heated and uncontrollable, and he told us in no mean French terms exactly what he thought of us. During this tirade, which lasted a full fifteen minutes, the two Afrikaans policemen were absolutely dumbfounded. They didn't understand a single word – all they knew was that all hell was let loose and deciding that self-preservation was the best form of valour slunk off into the shadows. Jacques was utterly right and when he had calmed down and I could get through to him I admitted it and promised never to do it again!

The children had a glorious holiday. Jacques' mother had died in Paris, so we brought out his sister's little girl, Annie who is the same age as Chantal, and we all came back by boat. This, of course, was a great experience for them. Not being the best sewing lady in the world I dug holes in my fingers making them all costumes for the fancy dress. Annie as Signal toothpaste – she won first prize – and Chantal as Brigitte Bardot, in a bikini with two of Jacques' socks stuffed into the bra! Shades of me doing my Mae West at the same age. I won the grown-ups one purely because having refused to dress up I was approached by a dear old General who had seen *The Love of Four Colonels* ten years before, and as there were three other real live generals on board, and as we had all aged a bit he asked me if I would accept to go as "The Love of Four Generals". I couldn't refuse *and* we won!

Derek Nimmo came back with his family by air, and went straight into *Charlie Girl* from where his career has soared to dizzy heights with all his television series, and I couldn't be more thrilled. I came back and went straight in to *Any Wednesday* at the Apollo.

This play was a four-hander with Dennis Price as my husband, Amanda Barrie as his mistress and John Fraser as her eventual lover. I loved doing it as it was a super comedy role for me. But we had bad luck the first week. Having suffered my own nervous collapse in Australia I was able to understand when a strange malady struck Amanda Barrie on the second night. Suddenly she couldn't walk. And couldn't appear the second night. And the poor girl was off for a week. This is the understudy's dream or nightmare. To take over on the second night must be just about the most terrifying dilemma for any actress. However, the girl who took over, an Australian called Monica Maughan made a great success for herself, and the applause of her brave attempt must still be ringing in her ears. Amanda came back and we had a very happy eight or nine months. It was during this time that I became inadvertently involved in a Cinderella who was to turn into a pocket millionairess. My dresser was a sweet girl from Cheshire. A country girl, with the makings of a "femme du monde". But she didn't know it. She had met a little Chinese student and they had fallen in love. She knew nothing about him except that his father had told him to look out for any Chinese antiques that he could sell in Hong Kong. They were walking one day in the King's Road and the boy stopped to look at a piece of Chinese bronze in the window. He was able to read the writing and realised it was an old piece and went in to enquire how much it was. One hundred and fifty pounds was the answer. He told the man to keep it for him and he'd be back next day with the money. The man didn't believe him judging by his appearance, and my dresser didn't think he had a hundred and fifty shillings let alone pounds. However, next day he bought his vase and wrote to his father in Hong Kong who said, "Well done, my son, if it's what I think it is, it's worth three thousand pounds. Send it over to me and I'll send it to the Boston Museum who are experts in Chinese *objet d'art.*" One week later the Boston Museum made an offer for it. It was a B.C., gold and silver chalice cup. Twenty-five thousand pounds was their offer. My little dresser was beside herself. Not only did her student now have twenty-five thousand pounds, but she discovered that he came from a millionaire Mandarin family in Hong Kong, who owned antique shops, airlines, sugar-cane fields, etc., etc. Now I bulldozed in and explained that if she were going to marry into all that, she could not arrive without any assets. So we set about getting some for her. The first thing we did was to learn Chinese. Every night during the first interval of *Any Wednesday* we would put a Chinese language record on and follow it in our handbooks. After eight months she was speaking fluently. She was able to practise at home. My family went into hysterical laughter every time I spoke so I didn't make much progress. Then I gave her some of my sure-fire recipes, because even if she was going to have a cook she must know her own onions, that is on the few occasions she wasn't going to be eating shark's fins or swan's nests! Then clothes. She had a pretty figure so we whipped up the bust, nipped in the waist and minimised her minis till she was floating. Hair and make-up and a few social graces and off she went at the end of the run, and had her engagement party at The Hilton in Hong Kong, and is now, I hope, living happily ever after. She invited me to go over to be best man or whatever it is but unfortunately I was working.

Chapter 16

IN the permissive society, which seems surreptitiously to have engulfed us, one of the art forms that has been most affected has been the cinema, and following close on its heels – the theatre. And now that the Lord Chamberlain has been laid to rest, stranger and stranger things are happening within London's erstwhile puritanical theatrical precincts. Nudity and eroticism are fighting for first place and gay old-fashioned things like homosexuality and lesbianism are served up as drawing-room comedies! I asked my agent what effect it would have on one's reputation and career if we accepted to do one of these strange plays. He answered quite succinctly that five years ago if one of his artists was asked to do a film with a nude scene in it he would have turned it down, but today he looks through the script and if there are not at least five nude scenes he turns it down! This preface is just to indicate how things have changed. Five years ago I did a play called *The First Fish*. It wasn't a good title but it was symbolic of being the first people (as we are supposed to be descended from fish!) to do something no one has ever done before. And the premise of the play was that I, the wife, whose husband has not been sexually stimulated and is becoming dull in every way, employs a "call girl" to whip him into shape, and from then on the wife is prepared to take over. Of course all the usual complications set in and it makes a very good comedy. But when we opened the press found the whole idea immoral and unacceptable. That was five years ago. Today they'd probably just find it dull. However, apart from the critics and the public in all the comings and goings of plays in the theatre, there is always the human side of the artists involved – a little point very often overlooked. We are more than just puppets, and although have the Pagliacci facility of "Laugh Clown Laugh" we are often very deeply affected by the people and environment in which we work. And in that play I had an experience I hope never to go through again. We opened at Richmond and my leading man was Paul Carpenter. And in spite of the fact that he had a very bad car smash a few weeks earlier, he seemed to have got over it and was giving a superb performance. As he lived near me, and his car was a "write off," I used to give him a lift out to Richmond every day. On the way to the theatre is a large cemetery and in it was the grave of his best friend, who was killed in another car crash, called Bonar Colleano. Every time we passed the cemetery he would wave and say, "Move over, Bonar, it won't be long now." But as he was in his forties and hale and hearty we would laugh and drive on. We were a sell-out at Richmond and broke all records. The public adored the play. And we were transferring to the Savoy. Paul was happier than he had ever been. Not only was he playing the best role he had ever played but he also imagined he was in love with me. As he had always been a very gay boy about town I didn't take it very seriously. But all the little attentions of a man in love were there. The flowers, the notes, the possessiveness and the protectiveness. His great joke was to present to me, with great panache, the tiny pieces of shattered windscreen glass which were still making their way out of his head.

One day just prior to opening at the Savoy we were rehearsing at the Vaudeville Theatre. Paul was called for three o'clock. And we left a message with the stage doorkeeper to tell him where we'd gone to lunch. He arrived at two-thirty feeling unwell and couldn't make it across the road to us, so got the key of one of the dressing rooms and went to lie down. The stage doorkeeper then went off duty. We returned from lunch, knowing nothing of all this, went on stage and waited for Paul to arrive. An hour went by and as he didn't turn up we had to abandon rehearsals. We all went home. What we didn't know was that Paul was only a few yards from us, dying and alone. When the actor whose dressing room he used arrived that evening for his performance he found Paul dead. Almost the most painful part, after the initial shock, was that because of the old theatrical and commercial axiom "the show must go on" we had immediately to find another actor to replace him. And within hours there was Ronan O'Casey saying and doing, very well, all the things Paul did. But the finality of it was almost unbearable. As if that wasn't enough I had another shock in store for me. A beautiful requiem service was given for Paul in the Catholic church in Hammersmith. He would have been so appreciative of all the theatre people who attended. There were a great many. He was a very popular man. As I was going out of the church I felt a hand on my shoulder. I turned and saw a man's face wich seemed only very vaguely familiar. He was very smartly dressed. As I was trying to determine who it could possibly be his violet eyes smiled and he said, "Long time no see!" Father Graham Matthews. "Well!" was all I could manage, and while I was trying to work out where his dog-collar was and how he'd changed and yet was the same, he was explaining he had left the church, and while he was talking I was only half listening because I was looking and wondering why I felt absolutely nothing. No "beast was stirring in my breast", he could have been a complete and utter stranger, and yet this was the man for whom I had tried to throw away my life. Tried to drown myself. How could it be possible that I could look at him now and have not one iota of emotion, just a deadness. It was like losing two friends in one day. How strange life and death can be.

And my life has settled down to running a home, my husband and my two children and a career. This is a pretty demanding occupation, but filled with so many compensations. Like the words of one's children reflecting one's own inate analogies. I was teaching Christobel, aged three, to say the "Our Father" and all went well until the line "Give us this day our daily bread". She repeated the line adding very firmly after it – "and CAKE!" Chantal aged five was taken as a treat to Mass at Westminster Cathedral as a change from our modest little church in Cadogan Square. "Oh, Mummy, what a beautiful church. This must belong to Jesus' Father!" Poor Jesus could obviously only afford Cadogan Square!

But I think probably the most memorable occasion was a children's party at Christmas a year or two ago. We had about forty children with all the usual amusements that London has to offer for these festivities. At Christmas-time I always put all the cards around the room on ribbons and a few "specials" on the mantlepiece. I noticed one rather grand nanny was perusing the cards, probably to see whether I knew the right people – or not! So for fun, I went to chat her up. Now every year Noel Coward sends a very amusing card. This particular year he had sent a picture of himself. On the front of the card was a schoolboy of fourteen complete with Eton collar, etc., and inside he had simply said, "Happy Xmas, *Master* Noel Coward." As we call him "The Master" in the profession this was an amusing touch! I thought it would impress the nanny, so I picked up his card and only showed her the picture on the front and said, "There you are, Nanny, there is someone you know." She looked at it and said, "Yes, the face is familiar, is it Lord Perth's son?" "No," I said, "Try again." "Oh dear, well now, could it be the Earl of Aberconway's son?" Well, I knew she wasn't going to get it, so I opened the card so she could read the words "Happy Xmas, Master Noel Coward". This she did and said, "Oh yes, I thought the face was familiar, well all I can say is I hope he grows up to be as clever as his father!" I told the story to Noel and he dined out on it for many months!

And talking of dining out, a few years ago we dined with Terence Rattigan, who wrote *The Yellow Rolls Royce*, in which

I played. My beloved husband, who is French and has an accent which is a cross between Maurice Chevalier and Yvonne Arnaud, and who is in fact a real Mrs. Malaprop, because he always gets the rhythm right, but never the actual words, and his knowledge of the theatre and its members is practically nil, was introduced to Terence Rattigan. He found him absolutely charming and fascinating but had no idea who he was or what he did, so when he left, Jacques turned to me and said, "What a charming man zat Clarence Rottingdean." Needless to say we've called him that ever since!

Another of his classics was when he had lent someone some money and I told him he was silly to have done it because he had no hope of getting it back. "Oh yes, I 'ave," he said, "I 'ave a 'I *know* you'!" And when Chantal was born he wrote to my family saying, "Poor Moira had a verry bad time, she had to have the baby taken out with TOOLS!"

With the exacting life of the theatre I find it indispensable to be able to come home to a completely different atmosphere. I can't live theatre or profession twenty-four hours a day. I need to establish the balance between the dream world of the theatre and the banality of domestic life. It is an absolute necessity to me to have them both. The scales don't work if an imbalance occurs. And in this I am indeed fortunate to have a husband who understands. It's no longer a question of finance or ambition or personal achievement, it is a basic requirement for my metabolism. If I am not working I become irritable, nervous and not very easy to live with. I am disorganised and muddled. But the moment I start to work everything slots into place. The household is properly directed, the children are organised and enjoyed and my husband is appropriately recompensed for his patience and love. And by this I *also* mean that I can cope with being his wife and hostess and entertaining his guests in the way he expects. But of course these moments are not always infallible even when I am on form. Two occasions spring rather disturbingly to mind, one when entertaining the Princess Bismarck, the other a party I gave for Maurice Chevalier.

The first was a seated dinner for twenty-four, and given in honour of the princess, which meant entertaining guests of her social level and cognisance. So the list included the Duke and Duchess of Bedford, whom she hadn't met but had expressed a desire so to do. The Duchess of Argyle, a colourful guest to say the least, The Kilmarnocks, friends of twenty years, Prince de Beauvau-Craon, godfather of Christobel and a childhood friend of Jacques, Prince and Princess Wiekersheim, the Duchess of Sutherland, Lord and Lady Ednam, Prince Murat, Duncan Sandys, etc. I only mention the guests to indicate the enormity of my embarrassment when things began to go wrong. Usually when I give a dinner party of this calibre I organise things to the minutest detail. I cook the food myself but arrange it so that I arrive in time trying to look as though the whole thing had been done by magic hands with no effort at all. Usually I have just put on my last eyelash as the guests are arriving. I arrange four tables of six, and hire a butler to oversee, and four footmen, one to serve at each table. I lay the tables myself and do the flowers, and when the staff arrive I treat it like a military operation with everyone given detailed instructions as to their duties. This is what usually happens. This particular night I had done my part. A really superb dinner, although I say it myself, had been prepared, and as I had put more effort into it than usual I was running a little late, and had not time to lay the tables. I had done the flowers and had put everything on the tables, place-names I printed in gold paint on ivy leaves, an idea, I readily confess, pinched from a fabulous luncheon in Paris I attended for the Duke and Duchess of Windsor given by Paul Louis Weiller at which were all the crowned and uncrowned heads of Europe. But as I had engaged five highly trained staff I decided that when they arrived at seven-thirty – dinner was at eight-fifteen – they could lay the tables and the butler would be ready to receive the guests at ten minutes to eight, and serve the champagne. Quite happily I dressed and prepared myself in a gorgeous dress and was anticipating a delicious evening of good food and sparkling conversation from my illustrious guests. Seven-thirty arrived and went, seven-forty, seven-forty-five, no staff appeared. I rang frantically to the caterers who were supplying them. No reply. Then desperation set in. I dashed down to the dining room, to try and lay the tables, got the children out of bed to help, Chantal, aged twelve, Christobel, aged four, plus nanny aged eighty, and *au pair*, aged eighteen. Knives, forks were flashing, napkins were frantically folded into tulips, glasses flashing on their way to their places – in the middle of all this the first guests arrived. No one to open the door. I composed myself, dignifiedly pretending it was just because I happened to be near the door that I had opened it. I rushed them upstairs into Jacques' bewildered arms, dashed down to put two more places at the table. Another couple arrived, same drill, and back to the dining tables. Third lot arrived. Again rushed upstairs, Jacques pouring champagne furiously and me pretending everything was fine, walking calmly out of the drawing room and the moment I was out of sight taking six steps at a time down to the dining room to lay two more places. So it went on until all the guests had arrived, the full twenty-four, and still not a sign of the staff. Now I was really desperate and at that moment the Princess in whose honour I was giving the dinner arrived. She was complete with Dior gown down to the carpet and along it, and long white gloves. I said to her, "You'd better keep your gloves on, dear, because you might just be serving the dinner." She laughed gaily, thinking I was making a very funny joke and having no idea how near the truth it was. So there I was with twenty-four people upstairs, a beautiful dinner downstairs in the kitchen, a now very pretty dining room with the tables all sparkling with silver and crystal, and absolutely no one to get the food from the kitchen into the mouths of my guests. Now here is where

The Very Merry Widow, Alan Melville style

Yul Brynner in *The Double Man* – he's no egg head!

The Very Merry Widow in action and How!

friendship really counts. With a streak of inspiration I rang the one friend in the entire world who could help. Charles Forté. I rang him and asked him to send five of his best men from the Café Royal to extricate me from my dilemma. Without a moment's hesitation he waved his wand and within the space of fifteen minutes five of his most experienced waiters, complete with black tie and tails, arrived at my front door. And my evening was saved. My guests had no idea how very nearly they were all given aprons and serving spoons and made to serve dinner themselves, which probably next season I will organise expressly in order to give them some fun. I have a feeling if they read this passage that I can expect certain refusals! I must just add that at nine-thirty p.m. the other lot of staff arrived saying feebly they were unable to find the house. I won't be explicit in the language I used to them but I can guarantee that, had they heard it, the eyebrows of my aristocratic entourage would have lifted off their heads. Needless to say, I have been kept in flowers of apologies from the caterers at monthly intervals ever since.

The second party was not quite so horrendous and the embarrassment only momentory, but nevertheless memorable. The number of guests the same, twenty-four, but this time it was purely a theatrical dinner in honour of Maurice Chevalier. And therefore I had invited members of our profession, who I thought would like to meet him and also would be fun for him. So there was Joan Bennett, Sir John Gielgud, Sir John Clements, Kenneth More, etc. Now I had tried to think of something really original to give them for dinner, as they are entertained so much. I wanted my dinner to be a meal they didn't have every night of the week. So my choice was Fondue de Bœuf Bourguignon. This is a meal which when prepared correctly is delicious and fun at the same time. It comprises squares of the finest fillet of beef, cooked individually by the guests on a fork at the table in a fondue casserole of boiling oil and butter and then dipped in a large variety of exciting sauces. As this is a dish which is not traditionally served in England – quite common in Switzerland – I gave implicit instructions during my military parade as to the order in which things were to be served. First the fires were to be put on each table so that the oil and butter were allowed to boil and would be just right by the time the meat arrived. Then the sauces immediately after the fires so that the guests could contemplate their compositions while waiting for the fillet, and last of all the plate of raw meat beautifully cut without a finger of fat on it would be placed in front of each guest so that all that remained was for them to spear it with their special forks, dip it into the boiling butter for one minute then into whichever of the myriad sauces took their fancy, then into the mouth and off into an appreciative daze of mouth-watering titilation of the gastric juices. So my twenty-four guests arranged themselves round the four tables, and on came the first course which was Bisque Homard served in large Abelone shells. Nothing could go wrong there. These were devoured and the shells removed and preparation for the next course was made. And to my horror the butler had got the order of things confused and instead of putting on the fires first, the sauces second and the raw fillet of beef last, on came plates of raw meat which were placed alone and unaccompanied in front of each guest. The reaction was *bouleversante*! Being well con-trolled and beautifully mannered, they tried awfully hard to look as though they ate squares of raw fillet of beef every night. Forks were toyed with, eyes watched each other to see who was going to put the first piece of dog's dinner into whose mouth. After the initial hiatus, conversation grew in rapid momentum – anything to fill in the time rather than have to eat what was put in front of them. Then just as I was about to rise and make a speech explaining that they were not actually meant to eat what was in front of them as it was served, the doors opened and in walked the butler and boys to install the fires and serve the sauces. So the day was saved. Of course after that, the relief was so great that I think the whole thing was enjoyed even more because of it.

So the trials of a hostess continue to harass and, one hopes, go unnoticed by the unsuspecting guests. But the reverse side of the coin was when I was a guest at a party given in a glorious restaurant in Athens. Jacques and I were guests of Jack and Margery Sangster on their yacht cruising round the Greek Islands. We stopped in Athens for dinner this particular night. We were a party of twelve. I have a passion for caviar, I confess cultivated in South Africa when I played *The Sleeping Prince* and the management, in pursuit of reality, insisted on serving me with real caviar every night in the dinner scene, for twelve solid weeks. After that I could hardly live without it! However, this night in Athens I heard one or two of the girls ordering caviar, so I jumped at the chance to order it too. When the waiter arrived to serve it, overcome with the anticipation and my mouth drooling, accordingly I ladled it out on to my plate, at which moment I felt the heavy hand of the waiter on my shoulder. And in my ear a harassed whisper, "The caviar is for *three*, Madame!" I looked down on to my plate and realised I did have rather a large helping. "I'm so sorry," I said, and started ladling it back into the now empty container nestling in crushed ice. I forlornly took a piece of toast and scraped the remains of little black eggs on to it as my eyes followed the glass bowl to the plates of the other lady guests.

Then, of course, there are the eccentric guests with whom one gets saddled unsuspectingly. When I did my film in Paris, *Mon Phoque et Elle*, I had a charming Englishman called Sir Campbell Mitchel-Cotts playing my father. When he told me he had raw eggs and brandy served to him at five a.m. in his bath before filming, I thought it was for laughs, but not at all, as I was to discover when we returned to England. He invited me to lunch in his luxurious apartment, filled with priceless antiques and pictures, together with three or four other ladies. We had got to the end of a delicious meal, when suddenly he rose from the table and said, "You have all been such good friends to me I would like to leave you all something in my will.

I shall telephone my solicitor to come immediately." And sure enough fifteen minutes later a bowler-hatted gentleman arrived with notebook and briefcase and sat down to take instructions. Campbell went round the table one by one. Hope Linnit I remember was asked which of the pictures she would like. She chose something unpretentious like a Degas. I was asked whether I'd like a lump sum or something each week. Being a realist I plumbed for a lump sum. Then he came to a lady for whom he obviously didn't care very much. He made no social disguise of his feelings and simply said, "I've never liked you very much so you get nothing." Poor lady in distress got up and left the luncheon party. And so he went round the table dispensing of his worldly goods while his solicitor took down his bequests. We all left considerably richer on paper at least. I often wonder at what moment he came to his senses and refuted the whole thing or whether this was a usual luncheon gimmick. Quite honestly I wasn't at all surprised when he did actually die a year or two ago, and none of us got a brass farthing. But after the luncheon that day I did return the compliment by inviting him to lunch in my home. He asked if he could bring Daisy. I naturally agreed thinking it was some lady-friend to whom he was attached, but in fact it turned out to be a pekinese. When he arrived with her in his arms he did have the grace to take her luncheon out of his coat pocket – a jar of caviar – explaining that all she took with it was a glass of champagne, and that she was accustomed to having her place laid at the table and on no account was the champagne (which I had to supply!) to be put into a bowl. She would only drink it out of a champagne glass. I must admit she behaved impeccably. Sitting with her paws very neatly on the table, savouring her caviar with the dignity of any duchess, and sipping her champagne without spilling a drop. My other guests were more than somewhat stunned but it was no use inviting eccentrics and not letting them indulge their little idiosyncrasies. He was a dear, sweet man, with many wonderful qualities –

that he was madder than the mad hatter was just one of them.

When we did our Greek Island cruise I was asked by one of women's journals to write a piece on my trip. So here are a few extracts from my article.

ATHENS.

"Being, as Portia might say, 'an unlesson'd girl, unschool'd, unpractised', my preconceived conception of Athens was, an ancient outpost of Europe basking in the glory of its former days, besporting the Acropolis, a quantity of broken-nosed statues and a great many ruins on a lot of sunbaked rock. But to continue the Bard 'Happy in this, I am not yet so old but I may learn'! And what a lesson!

"The approach by yacht is an impressive sight of a great sprawling city, dominated by the incomparable Parthenon with immense modern blocks which seem to be carved out of their native marble, where old and new seem to be blood-brothers instead of unrelated misfits.

"We have seen the Italian Miracle and the German Miracle and I would hazard a guess that we are about to witness the Greek Miracle. I had a quick word with the Oracle to see if she could see her way to fixing up a British Miracle! She seemed to intimate that a few more noses needed breaking first!

"I came to Athens, foolishly I thought, to get away from it all, but as far as I could see it is all here!

"We chose the Grande Bretagne because we couldn't pronounce the names of any of the other hotels, only to find it had become the Marienbad of millionaires. In its air-conditioned marble halls I caught a glimpse of the ravishing Soraya, trying hard to pretend she was not Soraya, but pausing just long enough to make sure she was Soraya! She was about to leave for the island of Mykonos, where Maximilian Schell was trying hard to pretend he was not Maximilian Schell – and pausing just long enough . . . but there, I am repeating myself!

"There was Stavros Niarchos in a great state of agitation awaiting the arrival of Princess Margaret and Lord Snowdon, debating the wisdom of having put a fence round his entire island to keep off sharks and photographers, lest Tony should arrive with too much photographic equipment, and that he, Stavros, should find himself the instigator of an 'Unfair to Greek Photographers Week'.

"We drove out to join some friends who have a cabin on the luxury beach of Astir. The sun beating down inspired a 'clams for lunch' campaign, so on with the masks and snorkels and little sharp knives and the whole party suddenly disappeared below water. When our plastic bags were filled with these delicious *fruits de mer*, and while we waited for the cook to prepare them, there was no question of sunbathing on the sand or rocks – No. No. – Nothing so pedestrian as that! We were each given a lilo with a little anchor, to lie on in the water, and dream of dreams; attached to it was a little cork bottomed tray which lay on top of the water and held the nectar of one's aperitif! What a life! From that vantage position and in a state of bliss and oblivion one could observe the hundreds of yachts basking in the midday sun like swans asleep. And far in the distance Onassis' *Christina* looking like a cygnet which by nightfall would be 'dipping deep for Famagusta and the hidden sun that rings black Cyprus like a sea of oranges'. (A poem I learnt as a child – I have no idea what it means but it sounds good.)

"After a fabulous lunch of moussaka and halva – and a two-hour siesta – I began to feel conscience-stricken about all those temples and statues, so with a guide book in one hand and a handsome guide in the other I hared off to enlighten my education.

"One of the most incredible pieces of work is in the museum – the fifth-century bronze statue of Poseidon, which was discovered as recently as 1928 at the bottom of the ocean. This is a most breathtaking statue. My guide asked me for a pound-note which I charily gave him, but to my relief, he used it only to indicate the remarkable stance of the figure. The artist conceived the action of Poseidon throwing the javelin and has sculptured him at the thousandth-of-a-second position with the weight of the body poised for throwing. The pound-note was passed under both feet to show that they were barely touching the ground and yet were so perfectly balanced that they carried the entire weight of this life-size bronze god.

"The museum was filled with treasures dating back as far as four thousand years. There were hundreds of tourists eagerly devouring the sight of so much treasure. One little American boy insisted on prodding everything with his ice-creamy fingers while his harassed mother tried to stop him. 'Don't do it, Dwight, don't do it, I didn't come all the way to Greece just to spend the rest of my life paying damages for you!'

"Having cursorily 'done' the museums and the Acropolis and deciding I didn't really have enough years left to me to learn a fraction of what there was to know about these great civilisations, the ghosts of which still seemed so vibrant, I felt I would nurse my inadequacies by indulging in a Greek tragedy played in its natural habitat. So in the shadow of the Acropolis and with the ruins as a backcloth and the star infested sky as a roof and the original marble seats of the open air theatre, I, with three thousand Greek enthusiasts, participated in the tears and tribulations of Andromache.

"It must be a great tribute to the joint efforts of Euripedes and Madame Synodinou that without understanding one single solitary word of what was being said I found the tears streaming down my face and contributing to the tumultous applause that burst like thunder out of the Grecian sky. When the applause had faded and the crowds dispersed and the floodlighting darkened, I stood alone in the empty amphitheatre. I looked up to the Parthenon which now was lit only by the full moon. I made a little vow to myself that this was only the first of a long series of pilgrimages that I should be making to this Mecca of the gods."

Chapter 17

Now a couple of films: *The Yellow Rolls Royce* with Rex Harrison and a yard long list of stars; and *The Double Man* with Yul Brynner and the discovery of two fascinating people. Yul himself and Britt Eckland, Peter Seller's ex-wife.

I was delighted to be given the amusing cameo I had in *The Yellow Rolls Royce* with such a glittering cast and the opportunity to work with and indeed meet a director I had always admired, Anthony Asquith. And I can't imagine why none of my friends in the profession had ever warned me of the kind of person Anthony Asquith was. First of all he always wore, while directing on the set, a very tired and worn, faded blue boiler-suit with an outsize leather belt, and on set he always sat on a camel's saddle! Well, sublimely oblivious of all this, I arrived for my first morning's shooting, never having met Anthony Asquith, and went to "make-up" and "hairdressing" at seven-thirty a.m. to be ready to be on the set at nine a.m. I was sitting under the drier at eight a.m. when there was a knock at the door and a funny little man with a bald head, no teeth and a faded blue boiler-suit arrived with a large bouquet of flowers in his arms. He graciously presented them to me and simply said, "These are to welcome you." I confess to my shame and humiliation I took him for the doorman, and said, "Thank you very much, just put them over there on the table," and I went on reading my newspaper. He did as he was told and left the room without another word. Imagine my horror when I arrived on the set and there was my "doorman" sitting in his camel saddle directing an intricate scene between Jeanne

Moreau and Rex Harrison. I could quietly have died of mortification. But great man that he was he rose above the whole thing, and pretended it had never happened. It was marvellous working with Rex. The results he achieved look so easy and debonair as though he breezed into the studio, said his lines and breezed out again, but what a revelation to see the meticulousness with which he worked. Scenes were repeatedly rehearsed. He was always word perfect before rehearsals started and anything extraneous was ruthlessly cut, until an economy of words gesture and performance was achieved, he was charming but at the same time demanding of perfection. I admired this immensely. Strangely enough Jeanne Moreau took the whole thing much more lightly, but she had a very quick facility for being in hysterical laughter immediately before a "take" and being able to switch to tears in a trice. She was fascinating to watch. Unfortunately Omar Sharif was not in my episode so I had no opportunity to see him at work but we lunched together and he had the same quiet depth that emanates from him on the screen. Bridge is his passion and that he'd talk about with enormous enthusiasm. So much for *The Yellow Rolls Royce*.

Then came *The Double Man* with Yul Brynner. This is an extraordinary man. Of gipsy stock, he started life as a high-wire circus performer, fell, when he was at the height of both the tent and his career, and rather than be relegated to being simply a "hold" man, got out. It seems he went into practically everything from guitar playing to nightclubs, to languages – he speaks about seven or eight – to being chosen for *The King and I*, from whence he has been enthroned ever since. He lives life to the full and then some. Tremendously vital, dresses to fit his station – viz. sports jacket, costing two thousand pounds, made of vicuna – enormous black Rolls with the windows all round of special dark glass so he can see out but you can't see in! Will take a year off from making money for himself and devote all income to distressed children or boys' clubs or underdeveloped countries. And as a contrast to him, delicate little Britt Eckland who I would say was just about as perfect physically as any woman could be – superb figure, lovely legs, super boos, hair, eyes, teeth, shape of face – everything, and with it a fun person. Sense of humour, modest, warm and it distresses me greatly that her marriage has come to a grinding halt. She seemed so right for Peter Sellers. Anyway, if I'd been a fellah I'd have carried her off on my white stallion any time.

It was while making this film that Alan Melville adapted a full-length comedy of his which was written while the Conservative government was in power, called *The Mallard Imaginaire*. But by the time the powers that be decided to use the play the government had changed and so the leading character had to be made a Socialist. This made the whole situation far more amusing because Melville was able to cock a snoop at the government by making his minister highly conservative by nature and upbringing, but of necessity highly socialist to retain his job in the ministry. So *The Mallard Imaginaire* was put on TV as a comedy playhouse piece. A duck comes in from St. James's and lays eggs in the Minister's IN tray. It went down so well that the B.B.C. decided to make it into a series of six half-hour comedies which were called *The Whitehall Worrier* which I did with Robert Coote. This involved getting into all kinds of wild situations every week. One filmed sequence we had to play out in the pouring rain and of course the only day they could shoot, naturally there was no rain, just a thick hoar frost on the ground, so undaunted out came the hoses, and the entire day was spent in the garden with frozen water sprayed over us. When one is trying to act and to look glamorous and a tiny icicle keeps forming at the end of one's nose and has to be chipped off by the make-up girl, it does become a little disconcerting. Another little bonus was a scene where I had to take off my mink coat and, having a bathing costume underneath, to show all those Olympic divers that it wasn't as hard as it looks I had to dive in the deep end and swim the length of an Olympic pool. Not only that, but as there were no facilities for resetting my hair, it had to be done in one take. I was terrified of making a fool of myself by doing a belly flop, so I insisted they get a stand-in who was a beautiful diver, and they could insert her dive instead of mine if I happened to goof! She naturally only had once chance too because of her hair. I made her go first so I could relax on my dive knowing we at least had one perfect dive in the can even if it wasn't mine. She poised, got the cue for action, took off, and did the most almighty belly flop I've ever seen – the entire pool groaned in sympathy. That was her one chance gone, and they certainly couldn't use that one. Now was my turn. I stood there trembling, saying to myself, "Just think you're Esther Williams trying to impress Johnny Weissmuller," and off I took and I think it's probably the only time in my life I've done a decent dive! Sheer fluke!

Then we had hamster trouble. The one we engaged, realising she was the star of the show, was highly temperamental and determined to take no notice of the director at all. So finally after battling all day to make her do what she was supposed to, she was ignominiously substituted by a stuffed one. And the rest of the cast developed St. Vitus Dance trying to pretend with little jerky movements that it was really alive and moving.

However, we had the greatest fun and lots of laughs and when that series finished Alan Melville decided to strip me of a perfectly good husband, all my worldly goods and mould me into a "Very Merry Widow". And if I do many more I can see a repetition of an embarrassing moment for my long-suffering husband comparable to the one at the Savoy Hotel last year.

It was at the party given by the *Evening Standard* for the yearly awards, which is always attended by all the stars of the theatrical profession. Our invitation had been sent to us as Vicomte and Vicomtesse d'Orthez, but when we arrived at the door, the red-coated toastmaster recognised me as Moira Lister, and when I gave him the card, so it would be easier for him to pronounce my married name if he saw it written, he got completely confused and in a very pompous voice announced, "La Vicomtesse d'Orthez and Mistah Listah!" So this year I should think he is quite capable of announcing, "The Very Merry Widow and Husband."

The title has caused quite a lot of amusement. For instance, at the B.B.C. television centre there is always a battle to park in the reserved area right in the front entrance as this is supposed to be only for V.I.P.s. As all the doormen are now used to seeing me going in and out, they very kindly let me go in the reserved area. But a new man was on one day and I thought I was going to have trouble. So very grandly I leaned out of my Rolls and told him I usually parked in the front circle. "Oh, do you now, well who do you think you are? The Merry Widow or The First Lady?" "BOTH," I said very firmly, put my foot on the accelerator and sailed in.

Almost every episode has had some unusual happening. The one where I had to pretend to get involved in a method school of acting doing Yoga and hang upside down from a trapeze. I have this awful habit of always saying "Yes" to doing anything without thinking what it involves. Hanging from a trapeze looks so easy, but actually it not only hurts like mad but every drop of blood rushes instantly to your head, so you are not only incapable of standing up when you get down, if you know what I mean, but you also look like an over-ripe tomato.

Then we did a sequence with animals. One animal is usually bad enough to try and act with, but, as I was supposed to be a veterinary surgeon's assistant and end up by taking them all home, we had a great dane, which slobbered all over me, ruining two dresses, an enormous bulldog whose normal breathing sounded so like someone snoring heavily in a great hurry that the sound department kept complaining no one else could be heard over this extraordinary noise, a Yorkshire terrier who gave little polite yaps just as I was coming to a laugh line, which killed all my gags stone dead! A French poodle whose best friend had sadly let her down about the niceties of deodorants. And just thrown in for good measure, two chimpanzees. The first was incredibly human and behaved like a spoilt child, it simply sat down and howled when it didn't want to obey its master. When I tried, with my best maternal instincts, to get it to come with me, it simply bit a lump out of my thumb! The baby one was enchanting with the slight exception that during the performance they had to remove its rubber diapers, and the sense of freedom proved too much for it, and it commenced forthwith to relieve itself all over everything, and everybody! Never let it be said I am not an animal lover, it's just I love my animals in small doses and preferably one at a time.

The episode we did about the two flats and me serving food to both of them at once was even more hilarious in actual fact than it was on the screen. First Beryl Reid is so funny to work with that hysteria set in pretty early. Then I got real baggles on the sole of my shoes so I actually skated from one door to another, and to crown all, to use the correct phrase, when I was supposed to pour the lemon mousse over my employer's head, the first time we did it the prop department had put too much gelatine in the mousse so that when I put the bowl over her head, instead of the mousse going all over her face and covering her, all that happened was her head made a nasty hole in the mousse. So we had to do it all over again, and this time they made it so gooey and slushy that her wig almost ended up on the floor. Poor girl, I felt awful having to do it to her but she took it all in good part.

One awful moment for me was when the whole climax of one episode builds up to my finding a cheque in the coffee jar which has been left by my lodger which saves the day and gets me out of embarrassing circumstances. Well, I have the most appalling memory for names, in reality that is. It is just a blind spot with me. I can work with someone for two years and one month later I can't introduce them to my dearest friend whose

174

name I also can't remember. People who know me accept this and are tolerant, but others get very hurt. However, we had done ten episodes and I knew perfectly well Donald Hewlett, who plays my lodger (I've just looked him up in *Spotlight*! Joke!!), was called Freddie, but Freddie WHAT? So we came to the end of the show and with a great flourish I had to take out the cheque and read, "One thousand pounds, signed Freddie . . ." and there was a deadly pause. I tried everything to think of his last name. Props could easily have written it on the cheque, but they hadn't and after what seemed to me an eternity, I let out a desperate howl, "I can't remember his name!" Of course the audience fell about. It got the biggest laugh of the show, albeit illegitimately, but of course we had to do it again. And this time I printed the name very firmly on the cheque! What would have happened if it had been in the theatre I don't know. Well, I do, because it happened to me and I almost ruined the thread of the play. It was during the *Kingmaker*, the big moment of my part was when I had to turn to Kay Hammond and say, "So you think you're going to be Queen of England, well, you're very much mistaken," but it so happened that afternoon I had been to see Vivian Leigh playing Cleopatra and was still very much in the mood of the film when I came on stage, I turned to Katie and stood my histrionic stance and with full blast of conviction said instead, "So you think you are going to be Queen of Egypt, well, you're very much mistaken!" It took me a long time to live that one down!

I am still the proud possessor of the scar where I was first blooded as the Very Merry Widow. It was during the mannequin sequence, when a very heavy steel dress rail was to fall on me and I was not supposed to be hurt, just embarrassed in a comedy way. We had rehearsed the scene many times and each time I asked Props if it was safe. They assured me it was. And I must admit it worked beautifully at rehearsals, but come the show with the audience, we got to the moment where I fall, which I did, and the rail is supposed to fall on me, which it did, and with such precision that it cracked open my head. I let out a pained expletive and was knocked out momentarily. As the stars I saw began to disappear I thought they would have stopped the camera, but not at all, it was still running and the audience were laughing fit to bust thinking it was all part of the act. So I had no option but to carry on. It was only when I got to the wedding dress bit that I discovered that I had cut my leg too and that the whole thing was covered in blood; when the episode was over I showed the audience my now red and white wedding dress. They laughed all the more and I'm sure thought it was tomato ketchup. So you see, you can't win!

We did one sequence actually in France, the idea of which was that I got a job with an eccentric very rich aunt of Freddie's, and the whole thing ends up in a disaster, I walk out without any money and have to thumb my way home, the last shot of the film being me on the Route Nationale with my suitcase trying unsuccessfully to thumb a lift. Well, we got to the spot chosen to shoot the shot, and I rather disdainfully said to Graeme Muir, who was directing, that we would not get any comedy out of the situation, because obviously as I was standing on the road in a very attractive brightly coloured coat, with my blonde hair flying in the wind, the first Frenchman to come past in his car was going to find me irresistible, stop his car and carry me off. So the gag of me having difficulty in getting home wasn't going to work if the first man picked me up. Graeme patiently said we'd try it anyway and see what happened. So I positioned myself very prominently on the main Nice–Cannes road with my little suitcase at my feet, put on my most welcoming expression and waited for all those gallant Frenchmen to fall over themselves to pick me up in their cars and carry me off, not knowing of course I was then going to tell them it was all for a film, and that they would have to drop me a hundred yards down the road. So I stood and waited. The first car passed, a man alone. I smiled; he never even looked my way. The next one, a man and woman, again I did my eyes and teeth act, the man smiled back but shrugged his shoulders in the woman's direction as much as to say, "Not with the wife in the car, dear!" The third car, again a man and woman, this time obviously a mistress because they were both gesticulating wildly and having a monumental row so that they were quite oblivious of the fact that I was trying to attract their attention. By now I was beginning to feel pretty stupid. A bicycle went by – my first success. He offered me a ride on the pillion – with great dignity I refused. The fourth car, again a man alone who shook his finger at me with a malicious smile as if to say, "Naughty girl, serve you right for being so wicked; if I wasn't late for my appointment I'd take the whole day off with you!" And so it went on, car after car to my shame and mortification passed me by, all of which was being taken on camera. I never felt so alone and unwanted in my life. What if I had really needed that lift? I was almost in tears when at last after what seemed like fifty cars ignoring me, one did actually stop, and as if to add insult to injury who should be driving it but our own Prop boys who had been sent to save me. My humiliation knew no bounds. All the crew thought it was terribly funny. I wasn't actually quite so amused. I couldn't wait to get home to tell my husband how his compatriots had let me down!

Many times when being interviewed I have been asked what has been my most embarrassing moment in my career. I have never dared tell this story before but I will steel myself and record it here.

During one of the episodes of *The Very Merry Widow* we were doing a pageant scene. This required the presence in the studio of a real live horse. Donald Hewlett's wife Diana is a show-jumper so she gallantly said she would bring hers from their beautiful Elizabethan home in Horsham. The recording day arrived and this quite superb, absolutely enormous horse arrived in our midst in the studio. Everyone was very impressed with it and made a great fuss of it. After the initial excitement of its arrival had subsided and we were preparing our bridge scene in another corner of the studio, Diana King was bemoaning the fact of how difficult to come by was real manure and she needed it so desperately for her roses. We all agreed that should the horse during the course of a long day "oblige" we would "save it for Diana". Word went round the studio and little buckets were placed in judicious places to await the arrival of this precious by-product! About an hour later I was roaming round the studio and I looked up and saw this magnificent beast standing at the back of the studio, and I stopped to admire it. As I was in the process of doing so suddenly I saw what I *thought* was manure descending in a large and impressive column. I gave a yell and shouted, "Quick, save it for Diana." All eyes immediately were riveted on the horse. The words had scarcely left my lips when I realised that I was looking at quite the wrong part of the horse's anatomy. I don't think I need go into more clinical details. Only that my embarrassment was more than acute when it dawned on me what it was I had given instructions to "Save for Diana"!! Needless to say that I have never lived it down and "Save it for Diana" became a catchphrase throughout the entire B.B.C.

But probably the thing I enjoy most about making *The Very Merry Widow* series is that it has almost become part of my life. Having the same people with me each week, going on set and finding my house that I know intimately, the same easy chair and settee, the same ornaments, the telephone in a place where I know where to go and answer it. My kitchen has become my own, even the coffee being in the arsenic jar doesn't confuse me any more. My girl-friends Diana King, Elizabeth Allan and Maggie Courtney have become real friends, and I suppose most rewarding of all is the audience identification. The amount of women who see themselves in my character and come up to me in the street and say, "My dear, we are so alike, my family say it should be me on the screen. I do exactly the same sort of things as you do!" And of course this is where Alan has been so clever in making my character a real one and the situations although comedy are really very possible. So that widows write to me and tell me of experiences they have had since their husbands died. Then, of course, there are the letters of proposals which I find very endearing. I'm keeping them because after all one never knows!! One gentleman was obviously so taken by one of the episodes that he sent me a parcel which contained a pound of tea, a pound of sugar, a dog leash, a bunch of buttercups (wrapped up in the parcel) and a cheque for twenty-five pounds! I kept the perishables but I did actually send him back the cheque. I felt it would have been cheating a bit to keep it. Which reminds me of perhaps one of the most touching experiences that ever happened to me, when I was going through a rather difficult time with problems of life and love and work, etc., which beset us all from time to time. I needed help and advice and I was spending the weekend in the country and went to Mass on Sunday, actually in the back room of a pub. And Mass was given by an extraordinary old priest who seemed to have an aura of a saint about him. It was difficult to describe but I felt terribly drawn to him. When Mass was over I said to my host, "I must talk to that man." It was arranged and I went back into his little room, which seemed so humble and impoverished. He looked half-starved himself. I knelt at his feet and he took infinite pains talking to me and giving me so much comfort and guidance that when I walked out into the sunlight I felt as if the world had been lifted from my shoulders. Shortly afterwards I left for Africa, but I was so haunted by his thin white face and deep-set shining eyes that I felt I wanted very much to do something for him. So I wrote out a cheque for quite a substantial sum, and posted it to him. A week or two later I received a wonderful letter from him full of encouragement and inspiration, and with it my cheque was returned saying he really didn't need it. But when I looked at it I noticed the right-hand corner had been torn off. There was a P.S. to his letter, "I hope you don't mind but I tore off your signature to give to my housekeeper who so much wanted your autograph and didn't have the courage to ask for it."

These are the wonderful reactions that come as a result of the work one does in trying to bring a bit of fun into the lives of the public and extremely rewarding they are.

I could go on and on, the stories are endless. There was the time in Tangiers in the Casbah when I was conned into buying a false diamond; the time in Corsica when our yacht was shot at by bandits; sailing round Stromboli in full eruption and the smell of sulphur so strong and the heat so intense that we had to change course and sail away from it. But I have to stop somewhere and maybe this is as good a time as any.

Chapter 18

WHEN I started writing this book I had no intention of publishing it. It was simply going to be a memory book for me to record some of the amusing and not so amusing episodes of my life. This is to me the great sadness of an actress's life that after twenty years of a successful career I have nothing tangible to show for it. Painters have their canvases, musicians their scores, writers their books. But our moments of glory are never recorded because they may happen at a matinée performance given for Chelsea pensioners, or on a bad Monday night when the house is not full. That moment may have been the performance that would have set the town and critics alight if one had been able to do it on a first night! But all we have are a few yellowing programmes, which tell us the name of the play, the theatre and the cast. So I began to regret I had not written down so many of the momentous occasions in my life which have coloured the canvas of my career (if you'll forgive the alliteration). So while sitting on the terrace of our beautiful sugar-candy villa that we have built on the blue Mediterranean, and looking into the sparkling ripples on the water, thoughts began to flow of how and where it all started, and as they unfolded I wrote them down and it was when I had got about twenty thousand words written that I was approached to have my life story ghosted and serialised, so instead of being haunted for four weeks (time required by ghosts apparently) I decided to finish it myself. Now that it is done and I read back on it all, it is almost like peeking in on someone else's life; because up to now I have never really looked back, always forward. Astrally speaking one would say that I have reached the halfway house in my cosmic life. I hope that I shall be spared to live through the other half because I think that the next thirty to forty years are going to be the most exciting that this earth has witnessed. Jean Jacques Schriver in his book *The American Challenge* has predicted such an advance in science that we are going to be left breathless. The computer age is upon us and has hardly started to manifest itself and when it does we are all going to be shot along at such speed that each day will seem that it has been started off with an early morning Concorde flight. All the established rules of life and living will be swept away and give place to a new and devastating whirl of existence. I look at my children and pray that they will be able to cope. But I don't worry unduly because this is their "Scene". Every new generation has had to learn to stand on its own feet and to adjust to its own set of problems. My rules were right for me but won't necessarily be right for them. But I sincerely believe that all the extravagances and apparent wildness of youth today is basically a healthy thing. They are casting off the restrictive crusts of a worn-out establishment, and trying to discover new dimensions. The initial result is to overplay their hands and become extreme, as we have witnessed in challenging theatre productions like *Hair* and others of that ilk. But as their music has already taken on a gentler mood, so I am sure will their behaviour, and I feel even more sure that they will emerge with a new purity and cleanliness of spirit which will be their own but will be valid enough to allow them to be absorbed into a society which they will fashion for themselves in a new and contemporary world.

For myself I cannot imagine what it will hold for me – other than seeing myself developing into an older and older character actress, until the day I gasp my last breath uttering some author's sacred lines, and am carried off stage and given a veteran's funeral! But actually I have to admit that I don't feel any older than the day I started. I review the future as an exciting challenge. There are still so many things that I want to do and see. There are never enough hours in any day to accomplish a fraction of what I have on my agenda for to-morrow.

We have built and designed ourselves this *petit paradis* over-looking the Bay of Cap d'Ail. The children are at school down here and I commute between London and France so as to continue the parallel of my two lives, without which I don't seem able to exist.

If I were to ask myself if I was any wiser after all my experi-ences the answer would probably be "no". I would say that the older one gets the more one realises how little one knows. How insignificant one's contribution. But this doesn't depress me. As long as I can continue to have the extreme good fortune I have had so far, am allowed to go on doing the things I love to do, have fun with my children, laugh with my husband, in short be thoroughly spoiled in having the best of all possible worlds, then I have absolutely no complaints and am quite prepared to sacrifice myself to this world for the next fifty years!

Notes

THEATRE

South Africa: *1929*   *The Vikings of Helgeland* (aged 6)
  „   „   *1935*   *Vintage Wine* with Sir Seymour Hicks
London: *1937*   *Post Road* (Queen's Theatre) with Louise Hampton, Mary Merrall
South Africa: *1938*   *Puppets Party*
  „   „   *1940*   *When We Are Married* (by J. B. Priestley)
  „   „   *1941*   *Passport to Limbo*
  „   „   *Our Flat*
  „   „   *Quiet Wedding*
  „   „   *Tons of Money*
  „   „   *1942*   *Escape from the Past*
  „   „   *The Women*
  „   „   *Victoria Regina*
England: *1945*   STRATFORD ON AVON SEASON (Juliet, Desdemona, Olivia, Kate Hardcastle, Charmian, Ann Bullen)
London: *1946*   JOHN CLEMENTS' SEASON (St. James's Theatre) with John Clements and Kay Hammond
  „   *Kingmaker* (St. James's Theatre)
  „   *1947*   *Marriage à la Mode* (St. James's Theatre)
  „   PRESENT LAUGHTER (Haymarket Theatre) with Noel Coward
  „   *1949*   *French Without Tears* (Vaudeville Theatre) with Robert Flemyng, Clive Morton
New York: *1949*   DON'T LISTEN LADIES (Booth Theatre) with Jack Buchanan
London: *1950*   *Sauce Piquante* (Cambridge Theatre) with Audrey Hepburn, Tommy Cooper and Norman Wisdom

London:	*1951*	THE LOVE OF FOUR COLONELS (Wyndhams Theatre) with Peter Ustinov
„	*1953*	*Birthday Honours* (Criterion Theatre) with Hugh Latimer
South Africa:	*1954*	*The Sleeping Prince* with Joss Ackland
London:	*1956*	THE JOHN GIELGUD SEASON – *King Lear, Much Ado* (Palace Theatre) with Dame Peggy Ashcroft, Claire Bloom, George Devine
„		*The Long Echo* (St. James's Theatre) with Joyce Redman, Denholm Elliot •
„	*1957*	*Paddle Your Own Canoe* (Criterion Theatre) with Nigel Stock
World Tour:	*1958/9*	ONE WOMAN SHOW – *People in Love*
London:	*1960*	THE GAZEBO (Savoy Theatre) with Ian Carmichael
„	*1963*	*Devil May Care* (Strand Theatre) with Ian Carmichael
„	*1963*	*See You Inside* with Amanda Barrie, Jon Pertwee, Harold Lang
„	*1964*	*The First Fish* (Savoy Theatre) with Paul Carpenter
„	*1965*	ANY WEDNESDAY (Apollo Theatre) with Dennis Price and Amanda Barrie
South Africa:	*1966*	*Bedtime Story* with Derek Nimmo
London:	*1967*	GETTING MARRIED (Strand Theatre) with Ian Carmichael, Alec Clunes, Raymond Huntley, David Hutchinson, Esmond Knight, Margaret Rawlings, Perlita Nielson, Hugh Williams, Googie Withers, Joanna Wake and Tim Carlton

FILMS

1945 *The Shipbuilders* with Clive Brook
1946 *So Evil My Love* with Ray Milland, Ann Todd
1947 *Love Story* with Stewart Grainger
1948 *My Ain Folk*
1949 *Another Shore* with Robert Beatty and Stanley Holloway
1950 *Uneasy Terms* with Michael Rennie
1950 *Mon Phoque et Elle* with François Perrier

1950 *Once a Jolly Swagman* with Dirk Bogarde
      Run For Your Money with Donald Houston, Alec Guinness,
        Joyce Grenfell
      Pool of London with Bonar Colleano
1951 *White Corridors* with Googie Withers, James Donald
1952 *Something Money Can't Buy* with Antony Steele, Patricia Roc
1953 *Trouble in Store* with Norman Wisdom
1954 *Grand National Night* with Nigel Patrick, Petula Clarke
1955 *The Deep Blue Sea* with Vivien Leigh, Kenneth More, Emlyn
        Williams
      John and Julie with Wilfred Hyde-White, Syd James, Constance Cummings
1956 *Seven Waves Away* with Tyrone Power, Mai Zetterling
1958 *The Agitator*
1960 *In Praise of Mary*
1962 *The Limping Man* with Lloyd Bridges
1964 *Joey Boy* with Harry H. Corbett, Stanley Baxter
1965 *The Yellow Rolls Royce* with Rex Harrison, Alain Delon,
        Ingrid Bergman, Omar Sharif, Shirley MacLaine
1966 *Stranger in the House* with James Mason, Geraldine Chaplin
1967 *The Double Man* with Yul Brynner

TELEVISION APPEARANCES

1948 *His and Hers* with Paul Carpenter
1949 *And So to Bed* with Austin Trevor
1950 *Bridge of Estaban*
      French Without Tears with Robert Flemyng
1951 *FRIEDA* with Derek Bond
1954 *The Bear* (by Chekov) with Henry Kendall
      FLOTSAM AND JETSAM with Philip King
1955 *NECKLACE* with Lyndon Brook
1956 *The Golden Cuckoo*
1957 *THE RELAPSE* with Peter Wyngarde, Jessie Evans and
        Michael Gough
1958 *DRAMATISED STORIES* (own series)
      DOROTHY PARKER STORIES (own series)
1959 THE JACK BENNY SHOW
1960 THE BOB HOPE SHOW

1961   *GILT AND GINGERBREAD* with Ian Carmichael
1962   *THE APPLECART* with Jack Hawkins
       'Find the Link' with Kenneth Horne and Josephine
          Douglas
       'What's My Line'
       'Juke Box Jury'
       'The Eamonn Andrews Show' with Mick Jagger and The
          Right Hon. Quintin Hogg
       Zero One with Nigel Patrick
       DANGER MAN (i) with Patrick McGoohan
1963   *The Golden Silence* with Douglas Fairbanks
1964   *SIMON AND LAURA* with Ian Carmichael
       'This is Your Life' Guest appearance with Petula Clarke
       'Call My Bluff' with Alan Melville and Ian Carmichael
1966   *DANGER MAN* (ii) with Denholm Elliot and Patrick
          McGoohan
       MAJOR BARBARA with Eileen Atkins
       The Mallarde Imaginaire (by Alan Melville) with Robert
          Coote
       'Going for a Song'
       'Call My Bluff' with John Gregson, Drusilla Beyfus
       'Juke Box Jury'
1967   *The Avengers* with Patrick McNee, Diana Rigg and Warren
          Mitchell
       THE WHITEHALL WORRIER (series by Alan Melville)
          with Robert Coote and Jonathan Cecil
       WORLD OF ONE-MAN SHOWS (B.B.C.2 colour) with
          Robert Morley, Sir John Gielgud, Joyce Grenfell, Dame
          Peggy Ashcroft, Dame Gladys Cooper, Michael Mac-
          Liammoir and Emlyn Williams
       THE VERY MERRY WIDOW (series by Alan Melville)
1968   *THE SEX GAME,* – *The Lovemakers* with Richard Pearson,
          Tony Bateman and Ian Dewar
       A TOUCH OF VENUS, – *Desmond* (one-woman play
          written by John Mortimer)
       THE VERY MERRY WIDOW (second series with Guest
          Stars Beryl Reid, Cicely Courtneidge and Roland Culver)
       'The Eamonn Andrews Show'
       'Dee Time'
       'The Monday Show'

1969   *THE DOLLY SPIKE* with Francis Matthews and Adrienne
     Posta
THE VERY MERRY WIDOW AND HOW (third series
    by Alan Melville)

RADIO

	1943	*Reading Own Story on Wartime Experiences*
		Just What the Doctor Ordered (B.B.C.)
	1947	'Insect World'
	1951	*Joseph Proctor's Money* with Robert Beatty
		Simon and Laura (series) with Hugh Burden
		Life of Bliss (series) with George Cole
	1959	*Blanco Posnet* (by George Bernard Shaw)
	1960	Reading Book of *The Inn of the Sixth Happiness* (The Small Woman)
	1962	'Five to Ten' Religious Programmes
	1965	*Merry Wives of Windsor* with Jimmy Edwards, Beryl Reid
South Africa:	1966	*Deep Blue Sea*
„ „		*Rain*
„ „		*The Millionairess* (by Shaw)
London:	1966	*Another Opening – Another Show* (own series)
	1967	'Be My Guest'
	1969	*Private Lives* with Keith Michell